The Place of Narrative in the Early Years Curriculum

The Place of Narrative in the Early Years Curriculum argues that children's ability to understand stories should not be underestimated. Using the results of psychological research, the author clarifies exactly what we know about how children develop narrative competence in the first eight years of their lives. It shows how this body of research can help us to understand just what it is that makes so many story books produced for pre-school children in recent years a success, and what deeper purposes they serve.

This book applies this research to day-to-day practice in pre-schools, day nurseries, schools and out of school play care settings. Offering advice on what works, the book shows how good practice based on practical experience is underpinned and clarified by research findings. Furthermore, it illustrates that an understanding of the development of narrative competence can challenge current ideas on various areas of early years practice, including child protection, health and safety and the consultation of children. Practitioners, researchers and students of early years education will find this a revelatory text.

Peter Baldock has worked with early years services for many years; as a community development worker, in registration and inspection, and most recently as a freelance consultant and associate tutor with The Open University.

The Place of Narrative in the Early Years Curriculum

How the tale unfolds

Peter Baldock

Routledge
Taylor & Francis Group

LONDON AND NEW YORK

First published 2006 by Routledge
2 Park Square, Milton Park, Abingdon, Oxon OX14 4RN

Simultaneously published in the USA and Canada
by Routledge
270 Madison Ave, New York, NY10016

*Routledge is an imprint of the Taylor & Francis Group,
an informa business*

© 2006 Peter Baldock

Typeset in Times and Gill by BC Typesetting Ltd, Bristol
Printed and bound in Great Britain by
MPG Books Ltd, Bodmin

British Library Cataloguing in Publication Data
A catalogue record for this book is available from the British Library

Library of Congress Cataloging in Publication Data
Baldock, Peter
The place of narrative in the early years curriculum : how the tale
unfolds / Peter Baldock.
     p.   cm.
Includes bibliographical references and index.
ISBN 0–415–38460–5 (hardback: alk. paper) – ISBN 0–415–38461–3
(pbk.: alk. paper)
1. Storytelling. 2. Child development. 3. Early childhood education.
I. Title.
LB1042.B344 2006
372.67'7–dc22
2005031146

ISBN10: 0–415–38460–5 (hbk)
ISBN10: 0–415–38461–3 (pbk)
ISBN10: 0–203–96952–9 (ebk)

ISBN13: 978–0–415–38460–5 (hbk)
ISBN13: 978–0–415–38461–2 (pbk)
ISBN13: 978–0–203–96952–6 (ebk)

For Tabitha and Emmanuelle

Contents

Acknowledgements

I have been helped in my work on this book by the comments on earlier drafts that I received from Janet Kay, Jill Lee and Rick Osborn and want to place my gratitude to them on record.

Introduction

A three-year-old child came home from her first visit to the cinema, where she had seen the Disney version of *Peter Pan*. She was used to cartoons on TV, but the sheer scale of the cinema experience had sent her into a fizzing excitement. Asked whether she had enjoyed it, she nodded vigorously. Asked to say what happened in the film, she replied, 'There was this man and the crocodile ate him!'

It goes without saying that this was an inadequate summary of the plot. Of course, the child may just have wanted to describe a scene that particularly impressed her. If you ask a ten-year-old to describe what happened in a film she has recently enjoyed, she is likely to be distracted by her excitement over the 'best bits'. However, if pressed, the ten-year-old will probably be able to give a reasonable synopsis of the plot. If the three-year-old is pressed, she will probably just become confused. The older child is able to do something that the younger one finds impossible. Why is this?

Something that can be called 'narrative competence' develops in the period that lies approximately between the second and the sixth birthdays. The term is borrowed from Fox (1993), although my focus differs from hers. Chapter 6 describes the concept in more detail. For the time being, a rough and ready definition – that narrative competence is the ability to understand and construct stories – will suffice. The central theme of this book is that this is an aspect of child development that is often underestimated but is of critical importance in curriculum planning, particularly at the Foundation Stage (the stage for children aged three and four in the British education system).

This may seem exaggerated. Surely, the ability to understand stories is just a natural consequence of learning to speak? To a large extent this is the case. However, it is true only because so many parents and early years practitioners help nurture narrative competence without thinking in those terms. One interesting piece of evidence for the fact that narrative competence does not follow automatically from general linguistic competence is provided by the experience of the action research team on Talking Time, a project designed to help children with lower than average verbal ability (Dockrell *et al.*, 2004). Those involved were less successful in relation to the children's 'oral narratives' than they were in other ways, a result that gave them concern. If narrative competence does not follow automatically from general linguistic competence, then some attention has to be paid to the ways in which it develops.

Reluctance to look at this issue rests on more than an assumption that there is nothing all that complicated about the ability to understand stories. They are not considered central to the life of the mind. At best, they illustrate in a casual, fuzzy sort of way the ideas that emerge more clearly in proper, objective thinking. At worst, they encourage fantasies that deflect attention from the real world. What, after all, does a grown-up mean when she accuses a child of 'telling stories'? It is something even worse than the wish to deceive. What seems to be implied is a frivolous attitude to truth itself.

This low opinion of narration has a long and impressive history, in spite of the fact that particular stories have been crucial to the self-image of every society. In Ancient Rome story-telling was a central part of the repertoire of professional popular entertainers, the *joculatores*, and there is a hint of how they were seen in the fact that the same Latin root lies behind the English word 'joke' and the Spanish word for a child's toy. The fathers of the Christian church believed that story-tellers were sinister as well as frivolous, describing them as ministers of Satan. That kind of sweeping condemnation survived into the early nineteenth century. While wholesale condemnation may be rare today, it is still the case that stories are often seen dismissively as a way of passing the time.

On the other hand, many educationists have seen stories as crucial. This is particularly evident in other parts of Western Europe, where the ideas of the Frenchman Georges Jean (1979, 1981) have influenced those of people such as Maria Emilia Traça (1992) in Portugal and José Manuel Trigo Cutiño and his colleagues (1997) in Spain. In the English-speaking world several arguments have been advanced in favour of attention to stories:

- There are those who claim that the fantasy element in many stories gives children the opportunity to explore and come to terms with feelings that are not easily articulated. Bettelheim's *The Uses of Enchantment* (1976) is a particularly well-known example.
- An alternative view, one that emerged at a much earlier period, was that stories that conveyed sound moral messages could provide a healthy alternative to fantasy. This started in the late seventeenth century with a handful of texts, such as James Janeway's 1692 account of the 'Conversion, Holy and Exemplary Lives and Joyful Deaths of Several Young Children', and reached a pinnacle in terms of sheer quantity in the early nineteenth century. At that point other, more secular, systems of morality tended to replace Evangelical Christianity, including commit-

ment to the empire. The use of stories to convey moral lessons is now well established and is a key feature of many books and TV programmes for children. The lessons being taught today, however, are unlikely to be about the imperative of conversion or duty to empire and are more likely to concern the importance of kindness and appreciation of diversity.

- A particular example of the use of stories for young children for ethical purposes is provided by efforts to interest them in traditional tales as a way of fostering knowledge of and loyalty to a particular culture. This was one of the factors behind the rewriting of folktales specifically for children in the nineteenth century. In the twentieth century the case for traditional stories was often made in rural regions of Europe as a protest against the dominant metropolitan culture. In the UK traditional stories from those countries that are the 'homelands' of many children now living here have been similarly employed as a means of enhancing the self-esteem of those children and creating positive images of Africa, Asia and the Caribbean.
- One final reason given for a positive appreciation of the educational role of stories is that, because children enjoy them, they can be a useful means of introducing them to various areas of the curriculum (Nicholson, 1996; Schiro, 2004; Teachers in Development Education, 2002) and can be an asset in the development of literacy (Grugeon and Gardner, 2000).

I have no problem with the idea that stories have a place in education for the sorts of reasons I have just outlined, although I disagree with some of the opinions of the authors cited. I have, however, two reservations. One is that the main focus is on primary school children and little is written about earlier stages of education. The second is that all the authors cited argue for a place for stories on the basis of their contents: it is what happens in stories that excites the imagination of children, offers them moral lessons, encourages pride in their various cultures, provides a way into subjects outside their daily experience or offers a reward for the attainment of literacy. In contrast, this book concentrates on the Foundation Stage (although I have some things to say about children before and after that stage) and also has a focus on the idea of narrative itself, on form rather than content.

Aristotle famously described man as a 'political animal'. He was not suggesting that all of us gain satisfaction from making speeches or doing deals in smoke-filled rooms. He was speaking of the fact that human beings live in organized societies. However, there are many species that have social structures and many of those have means of conveying crucial messages. What is unique about our species is that we use language to do more than give vent to emotion or convey brief messages. We are the only animals that tell each other stories. Understanding the development of that aspect of behaviour is a key to understanding the whole of child development and its implications for education.

This is not an original point of view, although I hope to develop it. The National Literacy Strategy appears to have established a more secure place for story-telling in primary education after a period of neglect that followed the introduction of the original National Curriculum. The Curriculum Guidance for the Foundation Stage says that by the time they have reached the end of that stage children should have learned to

> make up their own stories. . . . Use talk to organize, sequence and clarify . . . events. . . . Retell narratives in correct sequence, drawing on language patterns of stories. . . . Show an understanding of the elements of stories, such as main character, sequence of events and openings. . . . Attempt writing for different purposes, using features of different forms, such as . . . stories. . . . Find out about past and present events in their own lives, and in those of their families and other people they know. . . . Use their imagination in . . . stories.
>
> (QCA, 2000, pp. 50, 58, 62, 64, 94, 124)

This book spells out how these skills develop in the average child and how that development can be supported.

Because narrative is such a pervasive aspect of our discourse, it is easy to take for granted. This casual familiarity has to be disturbed before we can think about it systematically. The first five chapters of this book suggest new ways of doing so, drawing on three areas of research and theory:

- psychology
- narratology (a recently developed area of study focusing on narrative itself)
- the relationship between narrative and other modes of systematic thought.

Some of this may be unfamiliar to many early years practitioners, but that is the point of it. In particular, psychology and child development form part of any vocational course, but even then the emphasis is often on authors from earlier periods with particular interest in education, such as Froebel, Montessori, Vygotsky and Piaget, rather than on the more recent research on memory discussed here.

Using the material in the first five chapters, Chapter 6 below describes the concept of 'narrative competence' in greater detail and outlines the process by which it develops, especially in the third and fourth years.

The last part of the book relates that concept to a number of areas of practice in early years settings.

Chapter 1

Memory and narrative

Introduction

We rely on our memory to keep in mind the unique sequence of events that constitutes a story as it progresses. Without it the story would become a series of unrelated experiences. The narrator also relies on the ability of the audience or reader to remember many other things, from the meaning of the words employed to the significance in the shared culture of things to which the story refers. The connection between memory and narrative goes even deeper. It is not just that we can remember stories or remember things that help us understand them. Unless adversely affected by trauma of some kind, we have a memory of who we are ourselves that is inextricably narrative in structure. This chapter will consider several aspects of memory and conclude by describing the narrative aspect of consciousness.

Is memory a form of recording?

In the days when all wrist-watches had hands, there was a trick that psychologists often played on friends or new students. Someone would be asked to take part in an experiment. It would be explained that time was a critical aspect of the experiment and the person would be asked to check the time carefully on her own watch. Once she had done so, she would be asked to describe the hands on the watch. Most were unable to do so. It is not immediately obvious why this was so. The person would have seen the hands seconds before. In fact, she had been invited to examine them closely (although she was misled about the reason for doing it). If she had had the watch for some time, she had probably looked at those hands a thousand times or more. In spite of all that, the inability to recall the appearance of the hands accurately was commonplace.

A simple experiment such as this casts doubt on the way that memory is frequently conceived. We tend to think of it as something like a camcorder that records experiences and then stores the film somewhere. We recognize that the tape may decay or be altered. We retain, nevertheless, considerable faith in the system of recording. If we think we remember something, it must have happened.

The image of a camcorder suggests that this is a recent idea. In fact, it is a very old one. In Ancient Greece it was believed that experience created memories in the way that a seal or stamp left an impression in soft wax. This way of looking at memory is still persuasive to some. For much of the last part of the twentieth century it seemed to be supported by something called 'flashbulb' memory. People often claim to remember when they heard about a major event in great detail, as if the scene had been lit up by a camera flashbulb. The example commonly cited is that many in the right age group remember the exact circumstances in which they learned of the assassination of President Kennedy. The difficulty with this is that on the comparatively rare occasions when the accuracy of these flashbulb memories can be tested minutely, it emerges that many of the details are inaccurate. It seems that what is really happening is that people are constructing narratives afterwards because they want to underline both the significance of the event and their own participation in it as recipients of the news (Conway, 1995). They believe sincerely in their memory but, in shaping it to preserve it, they appear to have invented minor details rather than to have remembered them with particular clarity.

Memory of events is, therefore, a matter of construction rather than the automatic recording of experiences. Experience leaves impressions in our minds, but our memories go through some further processing if recall is to become possible. As long ago as 1932 Bartlett argued against the idea of 'lifeless, fixed and unchanging memory traces' (Bartlett, 1950, p. 32). Yet scientists were still attempting in the 1960s to transfer memories from dead rats or worms by feeding material from their corpses to others of the same species (Johnson, 1992). At that time evidence that memory is not an impression left on inert material, but something actively created, was limited. It has grown enormously since then.

Analysing the phenomena of memory and cognition

Difficulties encountered in the search for memory traces (or 'engrams') in the form of biological equivalents of camcorder tapes suggested that more could be learned about memory through the systematic study of how people (usually, as it happened, white male undergraduates) behaved rather than through biology. The systematic study of behaviour produced many discoveries on points of detail. What proved more difficult was to construct general models or even a terminology on which agreement was possible. This is partly because we remember different kinds of things. My memories of my own telephone number, of how to use a keyboard, of what I did yesterday, of the taste of seaside rock, of the face of an acquaintance or of what Jean Piaget had to say about child development seem to entail different kinds of experience. This is confirmed by the findings of research on the ways in which different kinds of memory are formed. We talk of a single faculty of memory, but this is at best a loose way of speaking. There seems to be a basic distinction between those forms of memory we can call to mind and think about 'consciously' and those that operate at a different level of consciousness, one that we share with other animals.

This distinction is only distantly related to the ideas of Sigmund Freud. In his conceptualization, the unconscious seems to have quite clear memories that are censored by the conscious self just as a dictatorship might seek to jam radio signals coming from the outside world. In getting through this system of censorship the unconscious adopts, as a spy might do, various disguises and finds its way to more conscious levels of the mind in dreams or in irrational behaviour that constitute metaphors for suppressed but quite explicit memories of events. It is a key element of psychoanalysis that memories in the unconscious are meaningful, even if largely inaccessible. This idea does not apply to the concepts of memory being discussed here. The approaches adopted by modern psychologists differ significantly from those of Freud. They offer no new reasons for seeing the mind in his terms, and at best are compatible with his views.

It would seem that all our experiences have an impact on us that leaves us with a form of memory which, without being fuzzy or imprecise, may not be preserved in an articulated, encoded form and cannot easily be translated into words. Think of a taste and then try to describe it. It is not easy, as any wine expert would admit. Of course, a memory that cannot itself easily be put in verbal form can be associated with recall of an incident. A taste or smell or some other straightforwardly physical sensation can evoke memories of people or places or events of which we are fully conscious, but such memories can be powerful even when they do not give rise to memories that lend themselves easily to verbal expression.

There are other kinds of memory, sometimes quite detailed, that do not come to us in verbal form. For example, someone who regularly travels by a particular route to and from work without any difficulty in remembering the way might have problems describing that route precisely to someone else without actually taking it again and noting consciously the information needed for directions. The laboratory experiments of Reber (1993) and others replicated this kind of experience many times. The controversy is around the question of how, if at all, this kind of memory differs from the memories of which we have well-articulated correlatives ('declarative' memory, in the jargon of psychologists). It is becoming clearer that both the creation and the retrieval of different kinds of memory can involve different regions of the brain.

The distinction between memories that are articulated and those that are not is one important issue. Another is the distinction between memory of the very recent and of the more distant past. At the end of the nineteenth century William James (1890) noted these two types of memory. Broadbent revived the distinction in 1958. In the decade that followed there was some controversy as to how the two kinds of memory were related, but it was widely recognized that we need to keep what has just happened in mind to operate at all in a changing world. It was also clear that this ability to keep in mind the immediate past might be different from the memories of the past that we can summon up consciously.

The phrase 'short-term memory', which was used by Broadbent, had drawbacks. It conjured up a picture of a temporary storage facility and it was clear that, if the idea made any sense, something more active must be involved. The term 'working memory' was widely adopted. It suggests the active construction of memories rather than the mere storing away of experience. 'Working memory' allows us to step outside the dominant present and see things that are happening in chronological perspective. It entails the creation of models of reality, often with a narrative form. It is these models that are then stored in retrievable form rather than the initial experience. The active process of developing them may help explain why first impressions count and it is sometimes difficult to erase from our minds misinformation we have once acquired even when we have the facts.

A number of models of working memory have been devised, of which the best known is that developed by Baddley (1986) and his colleagues over a number of years in the United Kingdom. This model has changed in development and has been contested (Andrade, 2001). Nevertheless, it has been very influential. The model comprises three main components (a 'central executive', an 'articulatory loop' and a 'visuo-spatial scratch-pad') and a description of how they appear to operate which has been subjected to empirical testing. It should be emphasized that the components are not different parts of the brain. This is a model of the mind, comparable in broad terms to the computer models others have produced. It appears to offer a reasonable description of what goes on in our minds as we undertake a task that entails keeping track of how a situation is unfolding. It has weaknesses acknowledged by Baddley himself. One is that it has little to say about the process of forgetting, an issue as central to the study of remembering as the formation and retrieval of memories. Another is that, being based on the observation of behaviour rather than on biology, it is limited in its ability to link sensory experience with the formation of memories. One of the interesting things about both working and long-term memory is that they do not appear to operate very differently in those born deaf or blind and in those who acquire such impairment early in life. Baddley and his colleagues recognized this in a significant qualification of their original terminology, putting the 'articulatory loop' in the place of the earlier 'phonological loop' and including spatial as well as visual awareness. The principal weakness lies, however, in the failure to describe more specifically the role and nature of the 'central executive'. It was this failure that led some to question the 'unitary' nature of the model on which Baddley has always been insistent.

At the time that Baddley was starting his career it was common to see the mind as a unified entity. To argue otherwise was to suggest a return to discredited nineteenth-century ideas of the structure of the brain and conflicted with the widespread assumption that each person has a single continuing identity. Fodor (1993) argues against the unitary model and makes a case for the existence of a 'modular' structure with 'domain-specific' systems for different aspects of cognition, each of which has 'computational' systems that are innately specified in great detail by the very structures inside the brain and that operate with a high degree of independence from the others. Any sensible model of the human mind is likely to be presented in 'more or less' terms and Fodor is naturally aware of the subjective experience of individual identity and, therefore, of the need for some kind of interface between these domain-specific systems. Nevertheless, his assumption is that there is a high degree of modularity and his ideas find support in the case presented by Chomsky (1968) that all human beings have a universal language acquisition device 'hard-wired' into their brains that allows them to develop competence in specific languages.

Fodor poses a potential challenge to the great majority of child development specialists who have assumed that the human mind is a single entity developing as the child grows older. Karmiloff-Smith (1992), a former member of Piaget's staff, accepts the importance of what Fodor has to say, but seeks to provide a model of cognitive development that moves beyond modularity. She challenges both the idea that modules are pre-specified in detail and the extent of the dichotomy Fodor sees between the modules and the final processing of material coming from them by the conscious mind. She describes a process of representational re-description which, she believes, accounts more plausibly for the way children progress in their ability to manipulate data than does Fodor's idea of modules or Piaget's notion of stages. It is a model that has much in common with those employed to design machines capable of learning.

Examining the brain

Experimental psychologists tried to construct and test models that would illuminate the ways in which we perceive our experience. This opened up new areas of understanding, but left controversies that it seemed would never be settled by experiments with conscious volunteers alone. There had been failures earlier in the twentieth century but it became clearer that there were strong reasons for looking for some of the answers in the biology of the brain.

A weakness of earlier neurobiology was that it depended on experiments or conclusions drawn from the behaviour of people who had suffered damage to particular parts of the brain or on experiments on animals that do not have the same type of consciousness as human beings. Technological advances made it possible to be more optimistic about the possibility of understanding memory and other aspects of cognition by examining the brain itself. Magnetic resonance imaging (MRI), positron emission topography (PET), near infra-red spectroscopy (NIRS), electroencephalography (EEG) and magnetoencephalography (MEG), especially when used together so as to avoid the disadvantages of each of them, have made it possible to examine what happens in 'normal' brains in some detail.

As a result of such techniques, and dissection and other work, we have a fairly detailed 'map' of the human brain, although, as Carter (2000) warns, it is a map comparable to those of planet earth in the early sixteenth century and there are areas about which we remain ignorant. Among these is the fact that we have only begun to explore the adaptability or 'plasticity' of the brain. We know from many sources that particular parts of the brain are linked to particular aspects of consciousness. We also know that this is not a neat and simple distribution of functions. The brain appears to have at least some capacity for compensating for damage. One reason for this is that different parts of the brain may be employed in the working of what appears from introspection to be a single system. For example, from experiments on animals it appears that some parts of the brain of a vertebrate may be essential to create memory and that they change physically when learning takes place, but in spite of this they are not required for the recall of memories (Rose, 1992).

The brain has a complex interior structure. The greater part of it consists of two hemispheres, each with essentially similar components. One of these is the limbic system, which is found just below the surface of the brain and comprises the amygdala, the hypothalamus, the thalamus and the hippocampus. The hypothalamus is the main processing centre for other regions of the brain and body, governing factors such as blood pressure. The thalamus is the connection site between the sensory components and the higher functions of the brain.

The amygdala is believed to be key to our emotional life (Le Doux, 1996). It is associated with our inborn disposition to feel fear or attraction when confronted by certain experiences and the development of that disposition into automatic reactions to quite specific phenomena. This would explain its close connection to the hypothalamus, which controls the body's fight or flight responses to danger. The amygdala assists us to learn from experience the appropriate response to stimuli. It is well known that events of great emotional significance can generate particularly salient memories, so that feelings appear to be associated with the construction of memories. In cases of post-traumatic stress disorder emotionally charged memories may be so powerful as to be disabling, but much of the time the role of the amygdala in fixing memories is helpful.

The hippocampus appears to be central in the processing of experiences into memories that are or can be made explicit, although it is not their storage place. It expands when the body experiences rhythm. This is probably associated with the importance of rhythmic sound and movement in facilitating learning. The role of the hippocampus in memory formation was not universally recognized until the early 1980s when a new consensus was marked by a symposium held in Germany (Seifert, 1983). Much of the interest in the topic came from observations of the major memory defects that could follow from damage to the hippocampus. However, there is still room for disagreement as it is rare in accidents to humans for the hippocampus alone to be damaged and some believe that damage to surrounding areas must have a role to play in explaining the forms of amnesia that often follow. There is widespread agreement that the hippocampus plays a crucial role in the consolidation of memory of specific episodes and it may have a role in the retrieval of memories of very recent experiences. Some argue that it is significant in the entire declarative memory system, while others give it a more restricted role (Kesner, 1998). The issue is important to the understanding of narrative competence, since the greater the role that can be established for the hippocampus in declarative memory, the stronger its role in the ability to construct narrative sequences. If Baddley's 'central executive' has a physical location, it would appear to be the hippocampus. It would be important if this could be securely demonstrated, since it would give the 'central executive' a more precise and modest role in the processing of memory rather than making it the site of higher-order consciousness, as some believe Baddley's model could imply.

The role of the hippocampus in processing memories means that it may also have a role in useful forgetting. At first glance it might seem that it would be an advantage to remember everything. However, those who have something like this ability often seem to be overwhelmed by it, unable to see the wood for the trees (Luria, 1969). Such people might have earned a reasonable living in the days of music hall and could still offer interesting evidence to psychologists, but their lives appear to be unhappy. We need to select the information we receive from the past and make patterns of it. Luria describes a patient who had difficulty following simple narratives, although he could remember, years after seeing them for a brief time, meaningless strings of mathematical symbols.

Computer modelling and connectionism

The primary mechanism of the brain is the transmission of information along neuronal pathways. The brain contains billions of neurons, constituting about 10 per cent of brain cell tissue. They have tendrils called axons, which reach out to make contact with other neurons via protuberances called dendrites. The tips of these, the synapses, can be directly linked to axons or can receive messages across any gap thanks to a chemical mediator called a neurotransmitter. Electrical signals transmitted between neurons are generated when stimulation of the receptors at the synapse leads to positive ions entering the neuron and altering its electrical charge. The brain operates on the basis of extremely fast and complex transmission of these electrical messages.

Early attempts to replicate this system in computer models had disadvantages, including the fact that it was unclear which aspects of the neuron were directly associated with memory and learning and the sheer number of transmissions in the brain itself. It was suggested by enthusiasts for the idea of artificial intelligence that, rather than attempt to replicate the structure of the brain, it would be better to design computers that could achieve what the human brain can achieve. It was the outcome that was important; the precise nature of the biological or machine structures that led to it was less interesting. However, the successes met in following this route were as limited (though also as real) as the successes involved in attempting to mimic the structure of the brain. Even if there had been more success, this would still have left wide open the question of how the brain itself operates. A machine capable of moving around safely on its own would be interesting and potentially useful, but might tell us little or nothing about the human activity of walking.

Interest began to develop again in ways of replicating what happened in the brain. A key to understanding this proved to be the appreciation that the brain is less like a computer (however sophisticated) than a computer network, with the neurons acting as individual machines in that network. Artificial neural networks based on simplified versions of what happens in the human brain have proved useful in many spheres (Gurney, 1997). However, it is still open to question how much they tell us about the brains they copy. Recent models are often based on what is known as the 'connectionist' approach, which stands in contrast to other models of learning in two ways. One is that networks built in this way do not involve accumulating pieces of knowledge in a dedicated part of the computer memory. Learning is a by-product of processing that involves changing the structures that drive processing itself. The other is that, in connectionist networks, knowledge is represented as patterns of activation distributed over many processing networks rather than as symbolically formed representations of what is known. This makes connectionist networks unpredictable in the sense that there is no algorithm that renders meaningful to a human observer the mapping between the microstructure of a connectionist network and the results it produces. This is what makes their learning much more like human learning (Cleevemans, 1997). Connectionism challenges not only some of the approaches that characterized early attempts to create artificial intelligence, but also models based on the concept of modularity. On those grounds it is given a cautious welcome by Karmiloff-Smith (1992), and is criticized by

Page (2000), who believes that a focus on the system as a whole risks inattention to the more 'local' aspects of consciousness. In Japan there has been work to devise new interpretations of dynamic neural activity in the hippocampus, using concepts from chaos theory to suggest ways in which episodic memories of quite specific events might be formed. These are ideas whose validation would be as much a matter of neurobiology as of testing the computer models that have been designed (Tsuda, 2001).

One approach to the whole subject that seems particularly promising is that of Edelman and his colleagues. He has outlined a biological theory of consciousness in a number of books, of which *The Remembered Present* (1989) is central, and has summarized his ideas in *Wider than the Sky* (2004).

Edelman's starting point is his notion of 'neural Darwinism', the idea that connections in the brain survive (or fail to survive) by a process similar to natural selection in general evolution. Those connections that are less helpful in the situation a human being faces will be relegated and may eventually atrophy through the failure to reactivate them. This represents a more dynamic picture than that which sees forgetting as a matter of memories fading away with time. In Edelman's model, consciousness arises when large neuronal groups form a dynamic core in the brain with connections looping back and forth between the thalamus and the cortex. In his later and more speculative books Edelman has tried to go beyond biology to speculate on how processes in the physical brain can give rise to subjective feeling.

Memory has a key place in Edelman's depiction of the mind. Consciousness could not exist without it. He specifies the complexity as well as the centrality of memory. It cannot be identified with the changes in the synapses that provide its basis. It is also unlike the standard memory of a computer. This should be obvious enough. If you are asked whether you wrote a letter to someone a year ago, you may be able to remember that you did. You could well need prompting to recall that fact or the gist of what you had to say. You are unlikely to remember the letter word for word. By way of contrast, your PC will contain either the full text of the letter or none of it. Computers, unlike human beings, do not have vague memories.

Memory in humans is, according to Edelman, inexact and based on associations rather than records of the kind that some have supposed the engram to be. However, it is inexact because it entails (in a healthy human being) a constant enhancement of the pattern-generating processes that arise from stimuli. The hippocampus links the categories we have formed over periods longer than the short-term present in which any animal lives. Thus Edelman believes that long-term (as opposed to short-term or working) memory is based on secondary synaptic changes that occur as a result of re-entrant activity from the hippocampus back to the central cortex. The creation of conceptual and symbolic mechanisms makes it possible for us to order events in recollection. Chronology is a key aspect of this symbolic ordering.

Our form of higher-order consciousness frees us from the immediate present and from learned simple responses to stimuli and enables us to construct pictures of the past and hypotheses about the future. Progress in this has a social as well as an individual dimension. Along with farming and writing, the most common aspect of a new civilization is the creation of ways of measuring time. The ability to step outside the immediate present also offers us a picture of ourselves as opposed to those things that are not ourselves. Edelman's theory attempts to go far beyond the question of how we remember things to the nature of consciousness itself.

General consciousness

Edelman is a leading figure. His theoretical approach is far from universally adopted, but it represents an important attempt to tackle a number of crucial issues and, in particular, the relationship between memory and the higher-order consciousness that makes human beings unique – at least on this planet.

Some object to Edelman's model because they reject any comparison between the functioning of the brain and that of a computer that is more than a loose analogy. Among them is the physicist Penrose, who locates the basis of consciousness not in connections between neurons, but in quantum mechanical processes within the neuron itself (Penrose, 1990, 1995; Langair, 1997). By way of contrast, Rose (1992), a biologist who has done important original research on the functioning of animal brains, criticizes over-ambitious claims for models which fail to take into account the environment in which the human being or any other animal operates. Meaning is not the same as information. It arises from a historically shaped process of inter-action between the individual and the physical and social environment. It could be argued that Penrose and Rose suggest ways of developing Edelman's approach rather than reasons to reject it.

The thought that our ability to remember things is not just one of the faculties that we possess, but somehow crucial to consciousness, is an un-familiar one. This is one reason why the importance of narrative competence is often underestimated.

The point is driven home by responses to experiments conducted by Libet (2004). In some of these, subjects were invited to lift a finger and report on the point at which they decided to undertake this trivial act. On average they reported an awareness of an intention to act 200 milliseconds before they did so. However, EEG readings showed that their actions began 800 milliseconds before their reported awareness of their decisions. In other words, they appeared to have begun to act before they decided to do so. This threw doubt on whether anyone could be said to be making a decision at all.

The experiments caused considerable dismay, not least to Libet himself, who devoted considerable time and ingenuity to further experiments designed to secure a place for individual free will. In some ways it is difficult to understand the extent of the concern. We often speak of 'making up our minds'. This process may take the conscious form of debates which we conduct inside our own heads on the merits and demerits of particular actions. However, if (as connectionists, such as Cleevemans, assume) learning can be implicit, there is no reason why we should be fully conscious of the process of arriving at a decision. Evidence that complex actions are not fully conscious is provided by the fact that those who have been fully trained in certain procedures can act quickly and effectively in appropriate situations, such as catching a ball in cricket.

The difficulty many have with Libet is that his work casts doubt on an idea of ourselves that is well embedded in our particular culture. Even those who believe that the mind is coexistent with the brain still tend to feel that there is a kind of little person inside who directs what the human being does. It is this concept that gets in the way of attempts to describe precisely the functioning of a 'central executive' in working memory or of consciousness in general. The idea of the little person inside is not universal. The ancient world often ascribed the actions of individuals to the intervention of the gods, who hardened people's hearts or made them fall in love. They did not look to coherent individual selves for explanations of what people did. Carey (2000) traces the modern concept back to the fifth-century African bishop and theologian St Augustine, who devised one of the first models of the human mind, one which provided the basis for the church's understanding of the individual soul's relationship with God (Augustine, 1955). Eternal reward or punishment for what people did in their lives on earth was justified on the basis that we possessed memory (as a sense of continuing identity over a lifetime), understanding (of moral choices) and will (the ability to determine our own actions). Augustine was also the author of what was arguably the first modern autobiography, focusing on his inner self rather than his public achievements (Augustine, 1960). Carey may have overstated the decisiveness of his influence, but he certainly played a key role and his idea of the inner self remains highly influential in our culture.

By way of contrast, the understanding that is implicit in much contemporary research on the mind is that consciousness of our own identities is something emergent, a reflection rather than an original cause of what we do. In that perspective articulate consciousness is a constantly revised narrative.

Conclusion

This chapter has provided a rather breakneck tour around several aspects of recent research on memory. It will be useful at this point to summarize.

- Memory has several forms and the connections between these are not fully understood.
- When we operate in the everyday world we have to keep in our minds an awareness of the sequence of events in the short-term present, in other words a kind of 'working' memory.
- What are called 'declarative' memories of the more distant past are not simple recordings, but constructions.
- We are still not clear how such memories are formed, although neuro-biological investigation, systematic observations of how people behave and computer modelling all have some clues to offer.
- There is an intimate connection (as Augustine first suggested) between our higher-order consciousness and our memory.
- Memory in that sense consists of constructed chronological sequences.
- Therefore narrative is central to our understanding of ourselves. It is not something peripheral.

What has been said so far has been about the healthy, adult human being. The situation of young children may be different. The next chapter deals with the way that memory, especially memory of events, develops in the first few years of life.

Chapter 2

The development of narrative competence in young children

Introduction

There is a psychological experiment you can try on yourself. Sit back. Get comfortable. Close your eyes. Relax. (No one is filming you or taking notes.) Now try to think of the very first thing you ever remember happening. It is important you think of an incident rather than of a place or a person.

If you have tried the experiment, the chances are that two things are true of the little story you have just recalled. One is that the incident occurred during the months around your third birthday. If you believe you can remember something that happened well before your second birthday, you may be very unusual, but the chances are that you are really remembering something in your very early childhood about which you were told later in life, with the story being made more memorable by photographs or the fact that you were still living in the same house or could see people or objects that featured in the episode. For most of us, the first event of which we have a real memory is somewhere between the second and fourth birthdays. For some it may be even later.

The other thing that is likely to be true is that you were at the centre of the incident (or at least the part you best recall). The attention of the others present was on you. Perhaps you were reluctant to admit this even to yourself because it seems a bit big-headed. The contrary is the case. The incident marks a key event in your dawning recognition that you are an object in the worlds of other people, just as they are objects in yours. It was – assuming that you have grown up to be a reasonably well-balanced person – the beginning of humility rather than of self-importance.

There are well-established terms for the two phenomena your experiment probably highlighted. The fact that few adults can remember much that happened before their third birthday is called 'infantile amnesia'. The ability of children to realize that other people have minds like their own, minds whose perspectives on things may be different, is described as their 'theory of mind'. Neither of these two pieces of jargon is particularly well chosen, but they are so well established that we are stuck with them. The crucial thing is the reality they describe, which is central to the child's development.

Memory in babies

At one time there was little research on the memory or general intelligence of young children, at least before their third birthday. This sometimes went as far as the suggestion that they had no power of recall at all. This was the product of ideas on education of the early eighteenth-century philosopher Locke, who saw the child's mind as a blank slate ready to receive, but in an entirely passive manner, the information that adults would write on it. His approach represented an advance in many ways because it supplanted the Puritan one that the newborn child was in the grip of Satan and had to have sin driven out, largely by means of physical violence. Locke's approach was gentler, but it did not recognize any kind of capacity in the child to do more than receive what was given. This led to a failure to appreciate the ways in which a child's cognitive abilities might develop. Locke's idea remained a dominant influence until well into the second half of the twentieth century and still finds expression in the impatience of some policy-makers in education with those who speak of the specific needs of the Foundation Stage.

In spite of Locke's influence, the failure to examine the memories of babies was strange. There were probably three explanations. One was that for much of the twentieth century some of the best evidence on how the brain worked came from studying the effects of brain trauma on patients. The statistical chances of a child suffering such an accident in the first five years of life were considerably less than those of an adult over the much longer period of seventy years or so. There were fewer such cases to study. A second reason was that most psychological research depended on the subjects of experiments reporting what they experienced. A child would not be able to do this before language was well developed. A third was that there appeared to be potential risks with most of the forms of brain imaging that came into use towards the end of the twentieth century. They often involved injecting small quantities of radioactive material into the subjects or placing them in magnetic fields. The evidence grew that these procedures did not cause harm if they were carefully controlled, but until that was so, there were sound ethical reasons for caution in using such techniques when dealing with people too young to give informed consent.

Things changed in the last twenty or thirty years of the twentieth century for several reasons. One was that the increasing excitement over neurobiology was bound to lead to interest in children as well as adults. Another was that technical advances made it easier to examine the mental activity of babies systematically. The geodesic net provided a convenient way of making records of brain activity. The rates at which babies sucked on dummies while undergoing experiences were reasonably assumed to indicate the level of interest in what was happening, and these could be monitored precisely. Confidence grew in the safety of brain imaging techniques. The third reason was that women academics who had found themselves gently pushed into the study of young children turned this ghetto into a base for interesting and novel work. Most, although not quite all, of the leading figures in the study of early cognition have been women.

There is now considerable evidence that memory develops from birth (or even before that, in the womb). Very young children do remember things, sometimes over long periods of time. The best-selling book by Gopnik and her colleagues (1999), who had themselves done much of the original research, brought the new evidence on the intelligence of babies to public attention. Before then the collections of papers published by Moscovitch (1984), Fivush and Hudson (1990) and Fivush (1994) had all shown surprising powers of recall in very young children. Perris *et al.* (1990) reported that three-year-olds in their study were able to remember things that had happened as long as two years previously.

Infantile amnesia

This mounting evidence led some to declare that infantile amnesia was 'dead'. The fact remains, and has to be explained, that most people cannot remember much before their third birthday. The evidence is overwhelming (Waldvogel, 1982; Pillemer and White, 1989). Infantile amnesia is not so much dead as poorly labelled.

If memory is seen as an accumulation of records stored in the brain, then forgetting what happened in the earliest period of life might be expected. Such memories might be overlaid by more recent ones, just as a new recording on a video cassette will wipe out what had been there before. The difficulty with this is that, while in some laboratory situations memories of information that has no meaning (random lists of letters, for example) do appear to become overlaid by new material, our recall of significant events does not operate in the same way. We can often vividly remember episodes in childhood, while forgetting a lot of what has happened in the recent past. Wetzler and Sweeney (1986) review evidence that the number of memories retained from early childhood is far lower than would be explained by average forgetting.

Freud (1953) suggested that the phenomenon arose from the child's need to repress memories that might be dangerous. This explanation stumbles against the fact that even the most innocuous or pleasant memories from the first two or three years of life appear to be lost. We might suppress the memory of a painful experience, but why choose to forget a happy day in the park or the first taste of a banana?

Another possibility is that until the third year the human brain is insufficiently mature to conduct the kind of processing required for episodic memory. Moscovitch (1985) believes this is the case. Both Nadel and Zola-Morgan (1984) and Carter (2000) suggest that the immaturity of the hippocampal formation may provide the specific explanation. There is some uncertainty as to when the hippocampus is fully mature. Moreover, while the available evidence suggests that a wider circuit involving the hippocampal formation is the substrate that makes long-term recall possible, it also suggests that the retrieval of distant memories in adults does not depend on the hippocampus itself, but on the neocortical association areas and the connections between these two. The neocortex develops later than the hippocampal formation and this may provide a neurobiological explanation of infantile amnesia. However, there is evidence that the required neural substrate is in place by about the time of the first birthday. Bauer (1997) in her review of this evidence suggests that the age of nine months may be the crucial watershed. Of course, it is one thing for the required neural systems to be mature and in place, another for the child to have begun to use them easily. Similarly, it may take a considerable time before the child who is physically capable of walking uses this as her normal method of moving around. It is still possible that further research on infant brains will identify a neural development that clearly explains infantile amnesia, but this is far from being the case as yet.

A different kind of explanation speaks of the development of precise cognitive skills and especially of language. Dokic (2001) speaks of the young child's lack of 'metarepresentational ability', an ability that adults usually possess. He derives this term from Perner (1991), who spoke about the fact that when adults recall something they are also usually aware of doing so. They see it as part of their own life story and experience. This is a more complex process than more or less automatic responses to things that are, for better or worse, familiar. Dokic believes that children do not develop that ability until the third year of life or thereabouts and that this explains why memories we may have of earlier periods have become inaccessible to us.

The idea that inadequately developed language makes it difficult for younger children to encode memories in ways that allow for later retrieval appears to make sense. Schachter and Moscovitch (1984) see it as the primary explanation of infantile amnesia. Fivush et al. (1997) see not only language in its basic form, but also the structure of narrative, as crucial to the ability of children to remember episodes from their past lives. They cite research evidence that children who are given narrative accounts of an event they experience while it is taking place or soon afterwards are more likely to remember it. However, it is common experience that children who are at the earliest stage of language development are able to construct and recall some memories. This cannot be tested rigorously in the laboratory, since evidence of such recall comes from children spontaneously re-enacting experiences that adults close to them know they have undergone. Never-theless, the anecdotal evidence is persuasive. It seems at least possible that children can construct some form of episodic memory before they can express it verbally. How far this is influenced by exposure to the language of those around them, which they may be able to understand before they employ it themselves, is a matter of speculation, although it is an idea that could be tested.

If explicit memories of episodes in the child's own life depend on the way in which these are represented for reflection inside her mind, then more than the availability of a large vocabulary is required. What seems to be impor-tant is the ability of the child to see herself in the episodes she remembers. This in turn could suggest the importance of her appreciation of the fact that her own perspective on the world is not the only possible one. At the beginning of this chapter it was said that your first memory of an event was likely to be one where you were the centre of attention and that this was related to the beginning of the realization that other people had minds like yours. The ability to remember experiences seems to be associated with the development of what is called the child's 'theory of mind'.

Theory of mind

The phrase 'theory of mind' had been used for a while by psychologists but was brought to greater prominence by Wellman (1990). Although the concept is relatively new, it relates to older ideas first advanced by Piaget (1960, 2002) in the 1920s of the young child's 'egocentrism'. This was not a moral failing, but an inability to see the world from any standpoint but her own. He believed this deficiency lasted until about the child's sixth birth-day. Both Piaget's research methods and many of his specific conclusions have been questioned subsequently. Nevertheless, he pointed to some decisive differences between the ways that adults and young children think. Further research (not to mention the common experience of parents and other carers) demonstrates that children in their second or third year of life find it difficult to understand that another person will not know what they know, but that this understanding is usually achieved by the fifth birthday. If a child of three is shown what appears (from the design work on the out-side) to be a box of sweets, is then shown that the box contains pebbles, and is finally asked to say what another person who is not in the room would think was in the box, she will almost certainly say pebbles rather than sweets. She has not developed an understanding that other people can see things from a different standpoint.

Empirical research on how the theory of mind emerges has underlined the importance of interaction with others in its development. Human children appear to be 'hard-wired' to interest in their conspecifics from birth and quickly learn to recognize a few familiar faces and voices. Thompson *et al.*

(1996) describe several pieces of research demonstrating the importance of mother–child conversation in encouraging the capacity for autobiographical memory in the young child. Other research has proved the importance of siblings. Cassidy *et al.* (2005) suggest that what matters is not interaction with siblings alone, but the precise nature of that interaction. They produced evidence that three- to five-year-old children who had siblings who were not their twins outperformed single children and children whose only siblings were their twins on various tests related to their theory of mind. Twins who had other siblings outperformed twins who did not. Children with at least one sibling of the opposite sex outperformed those whose siblings were all of the same sex. In other words, contact with a mind that is close in age, but different, seems to play a key role in producing the understanding that other people's minds are different.

The 'theory of mind' must be closely related to what Perner called 'meta-representation'. Once it is possible for a child to understand that other people have different perspectives on things, it becomes possible for her to achieve some kind of objectivity about her own, and to develop a more refined understanding of individual events as opposed to things that happen regularly. Thus the theory of mind is essential to the child's competence to understand where she stands in the world. She needs not only to acquire the word 'me', but also to appreciate that everyone is a 'me' and the word does not refer to herself alone.

Kleinknecht and Beike (2004) found a close connection between the performance of twenty-two pre-school children they studied in standard theory of mind tests and their narrative skills. They point out that the relationship between these skills is probably complex and that an understanding of the existence of other minds might both facilitate event memories (and, therefore, their retrieval as the basis of anecdotes) and also help them develop conversational skills so that others, especially close adults, find it easier to engage them in conversation. It is probably a matter of a self-reinforcing cycle rather than of simple cause and effect. However, an understanding of other minds does appear to be crucial to some aspects of the child's developing ability to understand narrative. Children develop some understanding of causation quite early in life (Gopnik *et al.*, 1999). This leads on to the idea of consequences of events. The intentions that generate events are much less obvious. Even children of six who have developed a theory of mind are most likely to fix on consequences as the important aspects of stories. By ten, children are paying more attention to the goals of the characters involved, as was indicated in the research by Stein and Glenn reported by Oakhill (1995).

A particular perspective on all this is provided by the spectrum of autistic disorders where children fail to develop a theory of mind in the standard manner. When Kanner (1943) first identified autism he described it as a failure of affect. Now it is seen as a cognitive disorder. Among the characteristics commonly found among autistic children of school age are an inability to understand the perspectives of others, problems with understanding that false belief is possible, a tendency to ascribe feelings and intentions to inanimate objects, and difficulties in understanding metaphor. All of these appear to be symptomatic of a failure to develop a theory of mind. Such children also tend to become seriously disturbed by change and are dependent on routine for both emotional security and their understanding of the passage of time. All these characteristics are also typical of two-year-old children with a reasonable grasp of language. Autistic people appear in some particular respects to be stuck at the stage of cognitive development of a two-year-old child. In the light of the subject with which this book deals, it is interesting that they will often have difficulty telling the story of a short film they have enjoyed on TV. They appear unable to construct narratives of any kind without the assistance of heavy clues (Loveland and Tunali, 1993).

Emily's monologues

A fascinating piece of evidence on what happens when a child has acquired a comparatively large vocabulary, but is at the earliest stages of narrative competence, comes from the detailed research that was conducted on a child called Emily in the 1980s. Emily was two years old at the time, very intelligent and with language skills more extensive than those of other children of her age. Like many two-year-olds, she often spent time after her parents had left her to go to sleep talking to herself. The idea of recording such monologues had already occurred to other researchers interested specifically in the development of language. In Emily's case her monologues were tape-recorded by her parents and then subjected to detailed analysis by a group of academics from different disciplines whose findings were published under the title *Narratives from the Crib* (Nelson, 1989).

Emily was just one child and her behaviour was observed rather than being tested in various experiments. This is the antithesis of most psychological research. Nevertheless, the material that came from the tapes is invaluable and sometimes surprising.

There was, for example, the unexpected fact that Emily had little to say about what might have been seen as major events in her life, in particular the birth of her baby brother, which led to her being moved to another bedroom to facilitate his care. Instead she concentrated on fairly routine events, such as her frequent trips to the library.

When Emily did speak about major events, it seems as though she was trying to shape them into routines (or 'scripts', in the psychological jargon). At 28 months and 18 days she spent some time talking about a (rare) visit to the airport. Rather than making this the story of an exciting episode as an older child might have done, she speaks of rules that have to be followed – taking luggage, taking 'something for the airport' (airline tickets?), needing a 'special' bus. These are all things she tells herself you have 'got to' do. Although she has clear memories of incidents in her life and spends much of the monologue time discussing them with herself, she is not rehearsing interesting anecdotes so much as attempting to create coherent universal guidelines. As she grows older, this becomes less important. She has grasped the most relevant guidelines. Thus at twenty-two to twenty-three months, when she speaks of a series of events it is usually a mere sequence. At twenty-eight months she begins to introduce some causal explanations into these sequences. (Interestingly, her use of words to mark the passage of time declines over that period.) At thirty-one months, after starting nursery, interaction with her peers there begins to be an important topic in the monologues. Dunn (1988) in her study of three-year-olds similarly found increasing numbers of references to other people in their descriptions of episodes. In view of the evidence of the importance of siblings in the child's development of a theory of mind, it could be significant that Emily had been an only child before the birth of her brother during part of the period in which her monologues were recorded.

It can be speculated that by the time she had started nursery Emily was beginning to develop both a recognition of the existence of other minds, like her own but not identical, and a greater ability to remember her own experiences as isolated incidents. She no longer needed to quite the same extent to use the narration of events to fight free of the detail and see a pattern. She had begun to see herself as an individual, needing to relate to others, having her own story and, therefore, able to benefit from hearing stories about other people. Bruner (1990) argues that for most human beings it is breaches of what he calls 'canonicality' (that is to say, what usually happens) that provoke narration. Emily's case and others, such as that of the two-year-old boy whose bedtime monologues are described by Kozulin (1990), appear to demonstrate that the canon has first to be established and this takes much of the first twelve months after a reasonable vocabulary is achieved.

Time

Autistic children have been described as 'lost in a sea of time' (Boucher, 2001). Learning to navigate that sea is as important as the appreciation of personal and historically bound perspective in developing an understanding of the world and this is also part of the child's cognitive development.

The routines that are so crucial to the two-year-old are based on the passage of time. To cope with these, the child needs to have some idea of past, present and future and some ability to use words such as 'then'. Even before the child develops an extensive vocabulary, an understanding of change becomes apparent. The game where something is thrown away, often accompanied by a single exclamation such as 'Gone!' with the obvious expectation that it can reappear, shows a dawning appreciation of change and of the possibility of controlling it. Freud observed the game being played by one of his grandchildren and saw it as an expression of emotional ambivalence (Freud, 1955). Gopnik (1984) speaks of the game as being important in cognitive terms, in the way it helps develop the child's concept of the permanence of objects even when they are not in view. 'Gone' is a kind of narrative, simple but apparently crucial in the child's developing sense of continuity and change, the basis of all narrative.

The sequential ordering of events is important in routines. A very young child appears to have difficulty comprehending sequence in any other context. This may be why Emily's use of words relating to time actually declined as she began to achieve the ability to understand chronological sequence outside routines. It will also be difficult for the child to think of what might happen as opposed to what normally happens. 'Like we usually do' was a recurrent phrase in Emily's monologues. Thus although Emily's parents often spoke to her last thing at night about what would happen the next day, this material rarely surfaced in the monologues and, when it did, it was as more material to fit into the frame of routine.

The ability to describe the usual routine for a day and sub-routines within it is something that most children seem to achieve by four years of age, six at the latest. The ability to do so depends on the extent to which there are established routines in the child's life. The behaviour of parents and other carers is significant in this, but other factors can come into play. For example, favourite TV programmes will be broadcast at set times, although the use of video or DVD and the repeat of the same episodes of many programmes throughout the day by TV channels catering for the pre-school child may sabotage this type of clock by dissociating TV-related experiences from particular times of day. At about the time that children acquire an ability to spell out the daily routine, they begin to pick up on what might happen in the future. It is at this point that children playing with each other will begin to plan their playing more effectively rather than simply responding to each other or aspects of the immediate environment in a free-wheeling way.

A good deal of work has been done recently on the ways in which children develop an ability to make proper use of their language's various ways of placing events in relative time. The evidence is ambiguous. The tense structure of verbs is one of the ways in which languages differ from each other most radically and tense is often not the primary way of indicating relative time, especially when the speaker is talking of an intention. For example, 'I am going on holiday tomorrow' is a perfectly comprehensible statement about a future event that does not make use of the future tense. The interpretation of the ways the child expresses past or future time is, therefore, complicated by the need to take different language usages into account (Bornstein et al., 2004).

It is well known to those who teach history at primary or even secondary level that children have difficulty in grasping long passages of time. Even adults have difficulty in understanding and speaking of long passages of time unless their education has instilled this skill in them. A sense of space (closely connected with a part of the brain called the caudate nucleus) seems to be present from very early in life. Our 'inborn' sense of time is less subtle. That may be why descriptions of chronological sequence over long periods of time are often more easily understood when presented in spatial or visual terms. Even in talking about their own lives, seven-year-olds struggle to describe a chronologically structured series (Engel, 1995b). Primary school children are aware that things happened before they were born but tend to lump the entire period before their births into a single period (John, 1989). A real appreciation of the expanse of human history does not seem to be developed until the age of ten or eleven (Steele, 1976), while a more abstract concept of time appears to develop after the thirteenth birthday in most children and as late as the sixteenth in some (Ward, 1976). Cooper (1995) disputes this, pointing out that much of the earlier research was influenced by fairly dogmatic versions of Piaget's concept of stages in cognitive development. However, when she speaks of overcoming difficulties by the judicious use of devices such as timelines, she acknowledges that the issue is there. Appreciation of historical time is a cultural construct and requires explicit teaching in appropriate ways.

Long before they begin to get to grips with the larger scale of human history children have to grasp duration on a smaller scale, but one that still reaches beyond the daily routine. This is not easy for them. Faced with a photograph or video film of herself as a baby, a three-year-old is likely to express disbelief that she was that baby, claiming 'I'm big!' Once she has accepted it, she may still find it surprising that her own mother was once also a child and may assume, until corrected, that one day she will be the same age as her mother.

Thus, although children appear to be able to remember things from very early in their lives, they find it difficult to recall episodes until they have developed a theory of mind and, alongside that, some notion of 'historical' time.

From routines to chronological sequences to genuine narrative

Because the focus in studies of children's interest in stories has usually been on the content rather than on narrative structure, few people have tried to assess narrative competence as an aspect of cognitive development. A major exception is the study by Applebee (1978), which examines how the child's concept of story develops from two to seventeen.

Among the material Applebee uses is some originally gathered from middle-class American children aged two to five years by Pitcher and Prelinger (1963) for purposes different from his. Applebee examines the extent to which the children's responses to invitations to tell stories make use of three conventions – formal openings and closures and consistent use of the past tense. He finds that even two-year-olds have begun to distinguish stories as a form of discourse, with 70 per cent of them using at least one of the conventions. There is a steady rise in this in different age groups, with all but a couple of the five-year-olds employing at least one of them and nearly half of the children using them by the age of three. The nature of the sample may, of course, have influenced the outcome.

Applebee also analyses six basic types of narrative structure in the stories told by the children. He finds that the youngest of them tend to offer what he describes as 'heaps', more or less disorganized collections of elements. These can only be described as stories out of courtesy to their authors. As they grow older, children tend to offer sequences, but these can be little more than better-organized lists with some new awareness of the passage of time. Eventually children begin to talk about events that are organized around a central situation. Thus there is an element that binds things together, but no real story. This type of story-telling develops into the production of what he calls 'unfocused chains' where each element of the story connects with the next, but the connection between the beginning and the end is tenuous. A child might tell of a cowboy who met a witch, then speak of the witch casting a spell on a third person, and so on. The child might make use of the phrase 'The end', but to an adult the ending might seem quite arbitrary. Applebee sees this as an important phase entailing some awareness on the part of the child of the possibility of different lines of development in a narrative. By the time the child is five the chains become more focused with some kind of central thread, usually a consistent central character. This in turn leads on to what he regards as 'real narratives' where there is a situation around which a story is developed, where there is often a climax of some kind at the end and where the ending is clearly connected to the starting point.

In defining these stages on the way to the ability to tell a story, Applebee speaks of two basic mechanisms at work – 'centering' (i.e. identifying a central element in the story) and 'chains' (i.e. that there should be links between the main actions in a story). He links what he has to say on this developing ability to the work of Piaget and more particularly to Vygotsky's ideas on the young child's formation of concepts. He speaks from an educational perspective and is particularly interested in these two theorists. He makes some use of ideas from experimental psychology, but his book pre-dated much of the material discussed in this chapter and the previous one. However, it is easy to see the relationship between his findings and those discussed earlier. His concept of 'chaining' connects with the idea that the development of sequences and routines is a crucial stage on the way to the child's ability to understand the world in narrative terms, while his concept of 'centering' links with later work on the theory of mind.

Conclusion

In what he had to say Applebee took for granted a concept of narrative. His interest was in the stages through which children must pass in order to be able to understand stories and even construct them for themselves. The next chapter deals with the concept of narrative itself.

Chapter 3

The shape of narrative

Introduction

The briefest survey of high culture or the content of everyday conversation will indicate the importance of story-telling. It might be expected that narrative, whether in prose or verse, would always have provided an important focus of study. In the sense that narrative frameworks have been identified as significant in literary criticism since the time of Aristotle, this has been the case. Yet, according to Oriega and García Landa (1996), Japan is the only part of the world where an advanced culture has seen narrative as such as a major literary genre. Certainly in the culture whose roots were in Western Europe, narrative itself was neglected in literary criticism until the last part of the twentieth century. Plays and longer poems that had a narrative framework were discussed for merits other than their storylines. When the novel had established itself as a literary form, there was still more interest in the light it cast upon society, in the values of the novelist and in the details of style, than there was in the narrative structure. E.M. Forster (1993), himself a famous novelist, described the story as a 'low atavistic form' to be valued only for the 'truth' and 'melody' that could be built around this basic structure.

It was not until the 1960s that the interest of critics turned decisively to narrative in all its forms. Although there were precedents (mainly from Eastern Europe), the impetus came from France. The word 'narratology' was coined by Todorov in 1969. A symposium held in Chicago in 1979 was a key event in providing the new discipline with an accepted place in the English-speaking world. In France, on the other hand, it secured a high status as part of a wider intellectual movement called structuralism, which sought to look beneath the surface details of an area of life and discover the basic structures that underpinned those details. When this approach was applied to the novel, narrative became central.

The search for a grammar of narrative

Todorov and others were interested in the possibility of constructing what they called a 'grammar' of narrative, a set of rules that would help explain how the deep structure of the story was transformed into the novel (or film or folktale) that was its surface. Before Todorov had devised the term, Barthes (1996) talked of analysing any narrative as a long sentence with a number of different levels. Such an analysis was to be based on a distinction between elements central to the plot and those peripheral, descriptive details that gave the story added interest and made it appear to be part of the real world where such detail could be found in abundance. The two could only be distinguished on the basis of a knowledge of the entire text and, in particular, of the way the story closed. It thus suggested a focus on the underlying logic of the whole rather than an attention to the way the plot unfolded. Bremond (1996) also spoke of a 'logic' of narrative and attempted to define the ways in which the sequence of events in a novel could develop in terms of the limited number of possibilities at each stage. He saw this as analogous to the way in which different sentences could be generated in accordance with the grammar of a language, which in some sense underlay all discourse that was conducted in that language. A similar argument was advanced in the English-speaking world by Fowler (1977).

It is easy to see the attraction of the idea that there might be a grammar of narrative. Language is made up of more than individual sentences and it is appropriate that study of it should take into account units larger than single sentences. In spite of this, the more that writers have attempted to refine the sets of transformations they see as underpinning the construction of narrative, the more bland and vacuous they have become. The most successful of the detailed grammars of narrative have usually been based on very brief narratives of two or three sentences (as in Prince, 1973, 1982), on narratives within oral traditions that have fairly rigid structures (a topic considered later in this chapter), or on modern formulaic fiction where action predominates. It becomes much more difficult to apply the idea to the novel that aspires to originality or literary status, whether this is the classic novel of the eighteenth and nineteenth centuries or more recent experimental novels. Barthes (1973) himself came to the conclusion that the type of analysis he had proposed, while valid, was too cold-blooded to describe adequately the experience of encountering a story.

There is nothing surprising about this. A brief narrative, lacking in detail, should be amenable to diagrammatic representation. A narrative characterized by strict conventions, however much invention goes into the detailed work of producing it, is bound by rules that can be loosely described as a 'grammar'. The novel, on the other hand, evolved as a form that escaped the boundaries of conventional literature. It has been constantly changing since the late seventeenth century and novelists of serious ambition have usually aspired to open up ideas, whether about literature itself or about aspects of the society they describe.

What, after all, would a narrative that failed to conform to the rules of narrative grammar look like? It would not be a mere jumble of incidents or reflections on experience. A random collection of individual words will not constitute (except by accident) a sentence that is structured ungrammatically. It is, however, easy to think of a sentence that is ungrammatical, but whose meaning remains clear, or of a sentence that is in grammatically correct form, but appears to be nonsense. A more fundamental problem is that there is a contradiction between the attempt to discover a timeless structure within a narrative and the intrinsically chronological form any carefully constructed narrative must take. Ricoeur (1985) demonstrates in a careful analysis of Bremond, Barthes and others the essential implausibility of the objectives of the structuralist writers on narrative.

The shape of a story

The attempt to construct a grammar or to discover the intrinsic logic of narrative fits uncomfortably with the fact that narratives are descriptions of chronological sequences. That issue had been present from the start. Todorov had taken as his starting point a distinction first made clearly by a group of scholars in Russia at the beginning of the twentieth century between the *fabula* (the events that make up the raw material of a story) and the *syuzhet* (the manner in which those events are recounted). Of Eastern European origin himself, he had been important in helping to bring this body of theory to the attention of the West through a book he published in 1965.

The distinction seems an obvious one. Any story describes a sequence of connected events, but the author may choose different ways to tell it. The narrative may be in the first or third person or may consist of what is supposed to be an edited collection of original documents (letters, press reports, etc.). It may describe what happens with or without comment. It may restrict the account to actions or may make extensive comment. It may start with the earliest event and progress steadily to the end or may summarize the plot and then explain it in detail, or it may start in the middle of things and then explain what happened before and afterwards.

The distinction between *fabula* and *syuzhet* seems reasonable, but it can be difficult to maintain in practice. Attempts to replicate narratives told in one medium in a different one (most frequently film versions of novels) tend to be unsuccessful. The manner of telling is clearly important. However, the events described do provide a key part of the structure in a way that attempts to identify a grammar or logic cannot take fully into account.

A common assumption in describing the structure of stories is that there must be a beginning, a middle and an end. A story must come to an end with some kind of climax that is logically consistent with the beginning.

The middle is the part where the process of alteration from the beginning to the end-state is explained. Ricoeur (1985) sees the ending of any narrative work as the touchstone of its unity. Kerby (1991) expresses a comparable opinion. For him the ending is not just a literary device, but reflects the fundamental way in which we seek to understand our lives. Brooks (1984) links the idea of closure in narration to the Freudian idea that each of us has a death drive, that we are driven to seek closure. Culler (1975) also speaks of the need to find a model for plot that recognizes the need for a sense of totality in which the closure plays a key role.

In many nineteenth-century novels the closure is comprehensive. David Copperfield becomes, in his own words, the 'hero of his own life' by the end of Dickens's novel. He escapes the shadow of his enchanting but ineffective mother, represented by his first wife, when he marries his second (who has, conveniently, been approved by the first on her deathbed). In doing so he achieves a balance of personality that reaches beyond the alternative male role models of his cruel stepfather and the dithering Mr Micawber. His own life is successful and he has the satisfaction of knowing that all those who have impinged on it in almost any way have come to satisfactorily good or bad ends according to their deserts.

There is something a little too neat about this. Real life is more complicated. The philosopher Iris Murdoch (1997) says that, since reality is incomplete, we must not be afraid of incompleteness. As a novelist she often ended her own narratives with questions. There are no events in life. It is a continuous stream. We create events when we structure parts of our lives as narratives.

Narrative takes us a step outside the normal flow of time. Novelists like Murdoch have been able to reflect the continuing flow of things in their work only because the novel comes in the physical form of a book which itself marks off its separation from the flow. A similar role is played by the opening and closing of the curtain in the theatre or by the use of titles and end credits in films. The fact that the beginning and end are marked in these ways makes it less essential to indicate opening and closure in the structure of the narrative itself in order to help the reader or audience understand that the story is something other than real life.

The move from descriptions of experience into more formal story-telling is essential. Fludernik (1996) argues the need to base narrative theory not on novels or other well-polished forms of story, but on what happens in ordinary discourse. This would, she suggests, provide a more 'natural' narratology. 'Ordinary' conversation is, of course, often characterized by utterances that are defective in terms of formal grammar. Similarly, the accounts of experience that arise in ordinary conversation, or even some written discourse, frequently lack well-structured plots. Thus in the natural narratology that she wishes to establish, plot would not have a necessary role. Her book offers a new meeting place between linguistics, psychology and literary criticism. However, in looking at the basis of narrative, she tends to underestimate the significance of narrative in the more conventional sense. Stories are attempts to analyse the world by extracting elements from continuing existence and giving them a form they lack in the continuing flow. They are as artificial as scientific theories. Our impulse to construct them is as important as the experiential base from which they arise. Thus the 'unnatural' conventions that govern narration are an important subject in their own right.

Oral traditions

This becomes clearer in the study of oral traditions of story-telling, which is one reason why the structuralists' attempts to devise grammars of narrative often looked to the work of two of the best-known writers about such traditions – the Soviet folklore expert Propp and the French anthropologist Lévi-Strauss.

Propp's reputation rests on his classic work *Morphology of the Folktale*, first published in Russia in 1928. In this book he analysed a number of traditional stories in terms of the 'functions' commonly found in them (Propp, 1968). 'Functions' determined the course of the plot. It was the type of action rather than the character or characterization of the person, animal or spirit carrying it out that he saw as important, thus overthrowing a number of earlier systems of classification of folktales. He identified thirty-one such 'functions' in the collection he studied and claimed that, while not all of them would appear in any one story, they always appeared in the same order.

Propp's work remained more or less unknown in the West until the late 1950s. Two people drew it to general attention. One was Dundas (1965), who, with the aid of a computer, used Propp's system to generate new folktales that appeared to be authentic. The other was Lévi-Strauss, who reviewed Propp's book and compared its approach with his own (Lévi-Strauss, 1984). Propp responded with considerably more anger than Lévi-Strauss's critical, but respectful, review might seem to warrant (Propp, 1984). Only a few years earlier he had been forced to recant the 'harmful cosmopolitanism' that had been detected in his readiness to compare Russian folktales with those of other nations. Anyone who was an academic throughout the period of Joseph Stalin's rule could be forgiven for being a bit edgy. Calmer reflection on the differences between the two might have followed, but in the West, and especially in the United States, the spat between them was continued with gusto by their self-appointed disciples.

Lévi-Strauss was a social anthropologist with a formidable reputation – a reputation that was based less on his fieldwork (of which there was, in fact, precious little) than on the theoretical approach he developed for the understanding of social existence, including myths and folktales. He claimed to have discovered a basic structure to the way that human thinking operated, one that was as valid for the most 'primitive' pre-literate peoples living in remote areas of the tropics as it was for Parisian intellectuals. We all tend, he argues, to think in terms of binary opposites (men and women, in the tribe and outside, raw and cooked food, etc.). All thought, including traditional stories and myths, follows the logic of this basic pattern. He invented the word 'mythologiques' to describe such structures (Lévi-Strauss, 1964, 1966, 1968, 1971). The idea is similar to Bremond's 'logic of the story'. Lévi-Strauss also sees stories as material whose underlying structure can be revealed by analysis, and even depicted in simple diagrammatic form. Any interest in the development of a story is, therefore, virtually irrelevant. Propp had been concerned with form and sequence when he would have done better to have examined structure. It is open to question whether Lévi-Strauss managed, as disciples like Pace (1982) claim, to have revealed something basic about the structure of human thought. He had at the very least shown up some thought-provoking parallels between the ways societies envisage things that are apparently quite different. However, his approach abolishes rather than analyses the specific form of narrative.

There have been others who have examined the practice of narration itself in predominantly oral cultures. In the period between the two world wars two Americans called Lord and Parry made a study of traditional singers of tales in the Balkans (Lord, 1960). The results of their research were published mainly after the Second World War and aroused considerable interest. Lord and Parry were initially impressed by the apparent ability of the people they recorded and interviewed to remember long passages of poetry. On closer examination a different picture emerged. The singer Advo Medović listened to a narrative poem he had never heard sung before and claimed to be able to reproduce it perfectly in his own performance. Recordings showed that, whereas the first performance had consisted of 2,294 lines, Medović's own had 6,313. He had elaborated on the original, for all his protestations that he had simply memorized it.

What seems to have been happening is that the traditional songs followed some fairly standard patterns and, moreover, sub-patterns were also called into operation within the general one by highly conventionalized cues and phrases. The rural Balkans of nearly a century ago may seem fairly remote from our society. However, Labov (1972) found a form of highly conventionalized oral narrative among young black men in the American inner city. This kind of shaping appears to be a product of non-literary narrative wherever it is found. Traditional forms of story-telling have been studied by the psychologist Rubin (1995) for clues to the way that the episodic memory operates.

The outcome of these and similar studies has been to strengthen the idea that the ability to remember stories is connected with both patterning and convention. This applies outside the realm of language itself. One of the most famous examples of impressive memory is that of Mozart, who, having attended a performance in Rome of Allegri's *Miserere*, managed to write out the score (which had been a closely guarded Vatican secret) with almost perfect accuracy. Clearly the overall pattern of the piece, together with Mozart's familiarity with the conventions that applied in the type of music Allegri had written, played a major role in this feat. The importance of pattern in music probably explains the phenomenal memory for score that many famous musicians, such as Toscanini, have exhibited. However, examples drawn from the world of music point to the importance of convention as well as pattern and this is confirmed by studies of narration. When Bartlett (1950) in his pioneering experiments on memory decided to test his subjects' ability to recall a story, he chose one from Native American culture because he wanted to avoid skewing his results by presenting them with material they might already know. In the event, the very unfamiliarity of the conventions that underpin the story he used seems to have had an undermining effect on his subjects' ability to retain memories of the story. Conventions in narrative rest on the mind's ability to recognize pattern, but the patterns most easily recognized are those that are well established in the culture of the person attending to the narration.

The law of three

Some conventions are, however, very widespread and the extent of their usage is probably an indication of how easy they are to grasp and may suggest something fundamental about cognitive processes. Among these is the law of three, which was first identified in a lecture given in Berlin in 1908 by the Danish folklorist Olrik (1992). He spoke of how many things came in threes in folktales and saw this as so common as to constitute a 'law', though he had little to say on why it should be so.

This pattern is found in a wide variety of cultural elements, not just traditional tales. In many religions three is one of the numbers signifying perfection or completion, for example in the Christian doctrine of the Trinity. In the late Middle Ages a number of subversive movements described human history as falling into three phases: the Age of the Father when men were ruled by the law, the Age of the Son when divine grace began to operate, and the coming Age of the Spirit when men would be free and in perfect communion with God. This pattern of history was taken up and secularized by a number of nineteenth-century movements. The most famous example is Marxism, which spoke of an era of primitive communism, which was overthrown by technical developments leading to social inequality and class struggle, which would itself finally give birth to the perfect communist society.

The 'law of three' is not sufficiently universal to be described accurately as a law, but it is found in many parts of the world and is widespread in our own culture. The fact requires explanation. It could be an aspect of the fundamental working of cognition that is so far not fully understood. Another explanation is that offered by Freudians such as Bettelheim (1976), who see it, predictably, as associated with sex. There may be some truth in both of these explanations, but it may be best understood as coming from a primitive notion of probability. Before more sophisticated forms of statistical theory were elaborated people probably thought in terms of an idea that was rarely articulated but could be expressed as follows:

> If something happens, it just happens. If it happens twice, it could be coincidence. If it happens three times, there is a pattern on the basis of which it is possible to make predictions.

Certainty and climax are associated. The early Christians were emphatic that Jesus had risen on the third day. One reason for this may be that in Jewish thought at the time someone who had been dead for three days could safely be considered dead rather than unconscious. Thus the reference to the third day underlined the miracle of resurrection. This is an example of the use of three to establish certainty. Three also designates climax. The Old Testament contains more than thirty stories where a victory happens after three days. The resurrection is in this pattern. The 'third day' is thus a theological rather than a chronological term, resonant of certainty and triumph (Schillebeeckx, 1983).

The pattern of three instances leading to certainty or climax can easily take narrative form. It is found in many of the tales adopted from traditional sources for children. Goldilocks tries three versions of three aspects of the house of the three bears – the chairs, the porridge and the beds – finding in each case the third one she tries to be 'just right'. The basic narrative shape having been laid down, it is repeated when the bears return. Everything points to the mathematical near-certainty of a young animal being in the house. There are three examples of three things being tried (certainty multiplied by certainty). Bettelheim (1976) sees the story as unsatisfactory because it ends with Goldilocks's disappearance rather than a therapeutic resolution of the conflicts over identity he believes to be the story's underlying theme. Others have found the ending morally disappointing. Several versions were produced at the beginning of the twentieth century in which Goldilocks returned to the house of the bears to apologize politely for her misconduct. None of these had any success with children. Goldilocks's disappearance is an appropriate ending because it represents the fact that the equation has been solved. Any attempt to describe what followed next (however worthy the motives for it) can only damage the shape of the piece. (It is also, of course, normal child behaviour to evade trouble if possible.)

The story of Goldilocks is a single example of a common variant of the law of three in which the third offers an exception to the pattern that is in process of becoming established. There are three wishes granted of which the third leads back to the situation before the wishing began. The hero is the youngest of three brothers (therefore the least likely to be successful) and he succeeds where they fail. This shape is taken by stories of various human heroes, of the three little pigs and of the three billy goats gruff. There is a similar pattern, although one less central to the story's structure, in Cinderella's defeat of her two stepsisters. The fact that the same thing occurring three times establishes a pattern allows the story-teller to create surprise (or at least a climax, if the story is familiar) by reversing the conclusion that the developing pattern appears to indicate.

This use of a three-fold pattern can be built into the form in which narratives are told. For example, among the Chinooka people (in Oregon) the basic song pattern is one of five-line stanzas where one line provides both the close to one set of three lines and the start of a second one, thus maintaining the flow of narrative while creating a series of climaxes within units of the song (Hymes, 1996). A similar pattern is found in the *Kalevala*, the traditional verse epic of Finland. It is also found in many longer pieces of music, ranging from some of the common patterns in the sung music of the Iggawin musicians in Mauritania to the classical symphony in eighteenth-century Vienna.

Story-telling in non-literate societies and with pre-literate children

Story-telling in pre-literate societies or those societies where literacy is a skill restricted to a minority often takes, therefore, very definite forms. The conventions may be broken but, when they are, it is usually in ways that are themselves conventional (as in the case of the third instance that reverses the pattern of the previous two instances).

In the nineteenth century many traditional stories became designated (usually in modified form) as suitable for young children and they continue to be successful under the misleading name of 'fairy stories'. There seems to be a close connection between the development of conventions in non-literate settings and the forms that work for children. This should not be read as an assertion that pre-literate societies are 'childish'. What is true of both oral story-telling in societies where this is a widespread practice and of reading stories to young children is that there are conditions that must be met to keep the audience happy. They must grab attention quickly. Their form must be such as to facilitate memory. The stories must show similarities in their form so that the pattern can be recognized quickly. The focus must be on the actions rather than the subjective experiences of the characters. The practice of traditional story-tellers and the findings of psychologists researching memory both point in very similar directions.

All narration depends on assumptions shared between the narrator and those receiving the story. Even at the simplest level the narrator relies on what the audience already knows to avoid having to drag down the pace of narration with detailed explanation. Take for example something that might be said in conversation:

> I had to take my car to be repaired. The engine was flooded. I drove into a dip in the road that was filled with water. I didn't realize how deep it was.

This is a simple narrative whose success as a communication depends on the fact that no one is likely to be misled by the fact that the four sentences occur in precisely the reverse order of the events. We might expect events to be related in the order in which they occurred, but we can use our familiarity with conventions of discourse (reinforced in the example above by any knowledge we have of the internal combustion engine) to cope if that order is not followed.

Complex assumptions are made when narration takes place. The person to whom the narration is directed always plays a part in its construction, filling in the gaps the skilled narrator knows can be allowed. Barthes (1999) is one of several narratologists who have described the active role of the reader, going so far as to speak of 'the death of the author', the individual whose message the reader passively receives. Both basic form and form specific to a given culture are important to the comprehensibility of stories. The child who has not had the time to absorb that culture fully needs simpler patterns and shorter forms in order to manage recall (Glen, 1978).

Conclusion

This chapter has been concerned largely with narration that is intended for an adult audience. The next one deals with stories that have been produced for children and some of their characteristics.

Chapter 4

Children's stories

The emergence and development of children's fiction

The idea that stories should be written specifically for children is comparatively recent and an aspect of changing attitudes to childhood itself. Many of the narratives we now think of as being essentially for children, from fairy stories to Punch and Judy shows, started life as adult entertainment.

The idea of children's fiction arose in middle-class homes where wives and children were not needed in productive labour and where Protestant commitment suggested the need to pay attention to the child's growing mind. One of the earliest and most interesting cases is that of Jane Johnstone (1706–59), a vicar's wife with three sons and a daughter, whose collection of home-made books and toys was discovered in 1986 and was described in two of the chapters in Hilton *et al.* (1997). What she wrote for her children is only moderately interesting compared with the fact that she did it in the first place. Hers is a very early example of women composing fiction for their own children and not seeking wider publication. Another, much later, example is provided by stories written by Mrs Corbet in the 1890s. There are probably examples today. This aspect of the lives of women has been largely lost to history. Men who composed stories for their own children or those of friends were much more likely to seek publication. Lewis Carroll's Alice books, the fairy stories of Oscar Wilde, *The Wind in the Willows* and *Peter Pan* all started life that way.

While the idea of children's fiction was taking shape, books written for adults continued to provide children with their principal source of stories. There is an indication of this in the case of novels like *Robinson Crusoe* and *Gulliver's Travels*, which are now published more often in abbreviated versions for children than in the original adult texts.

The major area of adaptation was the revision of what are known as 'fairy stories'. These usually started life as brief oral narratives circulating among country people. From the time of the Renaissance they began to be written down as entertainment for city dwellers. The earliest examples came from Italy with Straparola's *Le piacevoli notti* in the 1550s and Basile's *Lo cunto de li cunti* in the 1630s. Several of their stories have found their way into the popular canon. Straparola's tales were characterized by a refined eroticism, Basile's by social criticism, his heroes often being penniless young men who are victorious against vicious aristocrats and stupid peasants. These two themes can be found in the authors who followed them, sometimes together in the same story. 'Beauty and the Beast', for example, is the story of the sexual awakening of a young girl and a protest against the ability of the aristocracy to make claims on middle-class people such as Beauty's merchant father.

France was one of the first countries to translate Straparola. In the seventeenth century there was an eager audience for the mannered tale of sexual matters that could be appreciated by persons 'of quality' but was not so overt as to invite the wrath of the church. Madame Coulanges became famous for entertaining ladies at the royal court with such stories in the 1670s. In 1697 Perrault published his *Histoires ou contes du temps passé*, a collection that includes versions of 'Sleeping Beauty', 'Red Riding Hood', and 'Puss in Boots'. The Comtesse d'Aulnay's *Contes des fées* was among the earliest books of this sort translated into English and is largely responsible for the fact that such tales are known as 'fairy stories'.

The best-known example of traditional stories being written down is provided by the work of Jacob and Wilhelm Grimm. Their original intention was to transcribe the traditional stories known to their servants and other people as a contribution to the strengthening of German culture at the time of the conflict with Napoleonic France. The stories they learned from their sources were, like those of Basile, focused on social rather than sexual matters. However, their outlook was more conservative. While Basile gloried in the success of the individual adventurer, the stories collected by the two brothers often warned against excessive ambition, as in 'The Fisherman and His Wife'. When it became clear that the collection had a market among parents who wished to see the tales passed on to their children, Wilhelm Grimm modified the stories to make them more acceptable. Wicked stepmothers replaced abusive natural mothers. Christian sentiments were put in the mouths of characters. The collection was an established classic throughout Europe by the 1870s.

In England there was a good deal of interest in imported traditional tales, including the Grimm collection (a version of which was first published in English in 1823), many of Danish origin (among them 'Goldilocks'), and *The Thousand and One Nights* from the Arab world. Traditional English tales were also collected. Several of these, such as 'Jack and the Beanstalk' or the story of Dick Whittington, followed Basile in their enthusiasm for the little man who was victorious against giants or great men.

A further development, one that occurred mainly in Northern Europe, was the writing of stories with more or less explicitly Christian themes in which the central character died in the saddest circumstances, but with the happy ending of eternal life in prospect. Examples include many of the original stories of Hans Christian Andersen, the stories written for children by Oscar Wilde, and George MacDonald's novel *At the Back of the North Wind*.

The idea of adapting adult fiction for children also remained important. In the twentieth century it became common to produce children's editions (often unabridged) of novels that had achieved classic status, especially if they included significant material on the childhood of the central character, such as *Jane Eyre*, *Oliver Twist* and *David Copperfield*.

The borderline between adult and child fiction remains less than clear cut. Collodi's *Le avventure di Pinocchio* (1883) borrowed its key features from a work of classical Latin literature, *The Golden Ass* written by Apuleius in the second century AD. The first William Brown book was written by Richmal Crompton with an adult readership in mind. She only shifted her stance as she began to realize the books were being widely read by children. Tolkien always intended his *Lord of the Rings* trilogy for adults. It was the three-part film version directed by Peter Jackson and appearing in 2001–3, and the merchandising that followed, that caused it to be seen as a book for children. The first publishers of *Watership Down* were uncertain what its market would be and hedged their bets by producing simultaneously editions with two different covers, one designed to attract children, the other adults. The Harry Potter series has secured a growing adult readership.

In spite of this uncertainty there is still a distinct area of publishing for children, usually marked out physically in the separate shelves that contain it in any bookshop. It is common to date this development back to the work of an early eighteenth-century publisher, John Newberry. This attention to the role of a publisher who was only secondarily an author arises in part from the fact that the first major attempt (in 1932) to describe the development of children's books in the United Kingdom was by someone from a publishing family who was naturally interested in the energy and initiative Newberry brought to this kind of enterprise (Darton, 1982).

By the beginning of the twentieth century the separation of children's books from adult books had been substantially achieved with the development of specialist magazines and book lists, the readiness of authors, including famous ones, to write for this specialized audience and developments in printing that facilitated illustration, including colour illustration. At the same time a gulf was beginning to form between the world of adult and children's books as a result of the increasing frankness about sexual matters in adult fiction. The development of a separate world of children's books was taken further by the creation of the profession of public librarianship, which in the United States and later in the United Kingdom saw itself as having a mission to encourage serious reading by children. A highwater mark came in the period just before the Second World War. In 1936 the Library Association established the Carnegie Medal to be awarded annually to an outstanding children's book. In the same year the first edition of *The Junior Bookshelf*, a specialist review of children's books edited by a former librarian, was published. In the following year the Association of Children's Librarians was formed. Before affluence made it easier for parents to purchase attractively produced books for their children the profession had a significant influence it has never quite regained.

The idea of children's literature

'Good' books for children have often been seen in terms of children's *literature* and criteria have been established that may have relevance for children with well-established narrative competence, but are of dubious relevance to younger children. Penelope Mortimer, an author of adult fiction, declares that there is no such thing as a book for children, although – with a detectable sniff in her voice – she admits there might be room for books devised for 'illiterate under-fives' (Mortimer, 1980). C.S. Lewis, the author of the Narnia stories, had spoken earlier of the fact that a good story for children will appeal to adults (Lewis, 1980). He has been upbraided for this on the grounds that he was saying adults knew better than children what they should read (Sharit, 1989, p. 87). This was not what he intended. He was simply saying that their stories should be as good as those written for adults. His point was similar to that of a reviewer of Hans Christian Andersen's stories who said in 1875 that only a writer who could write 'for men' (*sic!*) was 'fit' to write for children (cited in Wallschlager, 2000).

The assumption is that children deserved fiction that was as 'good' (meaning as literary) as that on offer to adults. This indicates respect for children, but it takes for granted their literacy and narrative competence and is thus directed at older children. The assumption leaves little room for serious consideration of books produced for younger children.

The adult and child as readers

Children may have books of their own, but their autonomy in this respect is limited. Their access to fiction depends on the adults around them as role models who may or may not be interested in books, and as sources of books whether they purchase them as presents or provide them in educational settings and libraries. Before literacy is achieved children depend on adults as readers or tellers of stories. Adults are, therefore, important mediators between children and fiction.

Wall (1991) speaks of the way this influences not just the consumption but also the writing of fiction for children. She distinguishes between the book intended for a 'single audience' (the child), the book intended for a 'double audience' (where adults and children may see different messages or aspects in a book and be intended to do so by the author) and the book designed for a 'dual audience' (where adults and children are intended to undergo the same narrative experience).

She points to an important aspect of many children's books. For example, a good deal in the Christopher Robin books invites the adult reader to smile at the child in a way that would scarcely occur to children themselves. However, her three-fold classification fails to take into account the fact that childhood is not a single stage of life and that adults are intimately connected with their own childhood. Enid Blyton suggested that children liked Noddy because he was just a little bit more naïve than they were themselves (quoted in Tucker, 1981). Children of five are often scathing about the limited narrative of 'baby' books. The classics of children's literature often have their classic status because their complex attitude to growing up makes them appealing to adults. They continue to be purchased for young children by adults whose first meaningful encounter with them occurred when they were themselves older.

What has been said so far on the relationship between adults and children as audiences of stories written for children relates to Western culture. Things appear to be different elsewhere, especially where traditional tales are still told to 'dual audiences', with no attention paid to the fact that there are children as well as adults present. There is little research on the effects of this on people from different cultures living in the societies of the West. However, Hymes (1996) sees the differences in expectations about story-telling between the Native American and the dominant Anglo-Saxon cultures as contributing to the educational disadvantage of that minority group in the United States. Even without specific research, we can guess that something similar might be discovered if a closer look were to be taken at non-white minorities in the United Kingdom.

Comics, films, TV and video games

Oral story-telling is not the only form of non-literary narrative. Other forms are significant today.

Like reading, video and DVD give the audience a measure of control over the pace of reception of the narrative that listening to story-tellers does not allow. They also create new opportunities for interaction, although these have barely begun to be exploited. These newer media make the traditional relationship between author and audience and hence the domination of the author more problematic. This has led to their being condemned (perhaps especially by teachers) as threats to literacy. Such condemnation is unjustified. The little evidence we have so far is that television, for example, encourages rather than inhibits reading, among other ways by helping young readers approach complex texts with clear pictures of the basic narratives in mind (Browne, 1999).

Another (and older) form of non-literary text is the comic strip. This was invented in the 1830s by a Swiss teacher, Töpfer, and began to emerge as a form of children's entertainment in the United Kingdom some thirty years later, partly on the basis of German models. The 'speech bubble' was invented by Edward Ardizzone a century later. It was the crucial device that finally distinguished the comic strip from the heavily illustrated text. By the time of Ardizzone's invention, film narrative was well established and since then the comic strip has tended to reflect film rather than function as a truly independent form of narrative. The increasing use of computer imaging has also made it even easier for film to surpass the comic strip in inventive visual effects.

Although the number of specialized programmes and even channels for young children has grown enormously since the close of the twentieth century, we still have little systematic research on the effect of this on younger children. There are stories of individual practitioners making imaginative use of video to help three- and four-year-old children grasp the outline of narratives in a way that helps stretch their competence and helps them understand and come to love the books on which they were based. On the other hand, there is some experience that suggests that prolonged use of video games, even those designed for educational purposes, can shape the attention of the child in a way that inhibits the development of narrative competence. The natural mechanism of the brain which allows us to build new 'representations' from experiences that are similar to, but still slightly different from, those that went before can generate an addictive fascination with the possibility of constantly improving performance. This in turn can lead to a concentration on strategy as opposed to an overall narrative understanding of a sequence of events. The mechanism that worked effectively in more difficult times when new experiences were rarer and less accessible to our control, and when learning to improve experience could be a matter of life or death, can go astray when technical advance creates the possibility of narrowly focused learning. The boundary between concentration and obsession depends on context. Essentially the same psychological mechanism is at work in both cases. Children who become fascinated with particular computer games can develop considerable strategic skills, but seem to do so at the expense of their developing narrative competence. It is difficult to judge the separate influence of technology, however, because of the scarcity of research and the complicating factor that, on the whole, new technology appears to have more appeal for boys, who are already less interested in narrative as a way of extending experience.

Pictures and picture books

Another challenge to the idea of 'literature' for children has been posed by the use of illustration.

It is one of the fascinating facts about the human mind that, from a very early age, children can understand and appreciate pictures. Pictures differ from reality in many ways. Even a photograph is two-dimensional and in that sense unrealistic. This demonstrates how significant an aspect of the human mind the urge to create and look at pictures must really be.

Illustration was an aspect of children's books from the start. In part this was because it was also an aspect of adult fiction. Illustrators, such as Cruikshank, in the early part of the nineteenth century drew for both children's books and adult novels and histories. It was only in the twentieth century (with the emergence of other forms of picture narrative) that illustrations tended to disappear from adult texts. They are still important in newspapers and popular magazines.

There exists a degree of hostility to the use of illustration in children's books. Goldthwaite (1980) claims they discourage the development of literacy. Protheroe (1992) believes that picture story books positively promote illiteracy. But in recent years several writers have taken a more enthusiastic view of picture story books (Watson and Styles, 1996; Evans, 1998; Cotton, 2000; Lewis, 2001; Arzipe and Styles, 2003). Ironically, while pleading the importance of picture story books, these writers often take a distinctly literary turn, talking of post-modernism and the advantages of semiotic text analysis in the study of illustration. It is as though they were over-conscious of the criticism that pictures can be seen as less serious than text and wished to compensate. At any rate, most of what they have to say concerns children well into their primary school careers and, like most writers on children's literature, they have little to say specifically about the pre-school child.

In spite of this they have performed a useful service for the understanding of books designed for younger children because they point out that pictures as well as verbal texts have to be read and that there are skills entailed in this. A child faced with a series of pictures, such as those in *The Snowman*, may see them as a mere series and fail to appreciate that they represent a number of closely linked events. Even when confronted by a fairly simple series (such as the one Wood, 1998, describes), a child whose narrative competence is not yet well established may have difficulty perceiving the 'centre' and, if asked to describe what is happening, may explain what the most active person in each frame is doing and fail to develop a story around the central character.

This may seem peculiar or amusing. We should appreciate that it is the result of the child's lack of familiarity with a particular convention. An adult who knows nothing about medieval art, seeing for the first time one of the great altarpieces in Sienna where the same figures appear in different parts of the painting, may have considerable difficulty working out what is going on until the conventions of this type of narration are explained. Adults read comic strips with ease because they know the rules. They do so even when those rules appear counter-intuitive. Comics produced in countries where writing runs from right to left have, nevertheless, retained the left-to-right convention of the Western comic strip. This is probably because the first comics ever published in Asia were translated versions of British or American originals.

The reservations, if not hostile criticism, about picture books in the world of adults are not reflected among children themselves, as anyone who has read picture story books with young children will know. Arzipe and Styles (2003) quote a five-year-old child saying that she always remembers pictures more than words. Lewis Carroll's Alice, whose observations are always acute, believed that a book without pictures was useless. It is doubtful whether the Noddy stories would have had quite the same success had it not been for the skill with which the characters were visually realized by the illustrator Harmsen van der Beek.

As many of the evaluations of picture story books observe, interest in pictures remains once literacy is achieved. It is not confined to an earlier stage nor does it threaten to keep children at that stage. Late in my own childhood, when I was given one of the editions of classic adult novels packaged for children by Dean publishers I always looked at the illustrations first, even though they were usually pretty uninspired watercolours. My two favourite books at the age of ten were loved because of the line drawings they included. In one case I cannot remember the name of the author, but I can remember that of the illustrator.

The authors whose evaluation of picture books is positive have stressed the potential of the marriage of text and illustration. Perhaps the most obvious example of such a marriage is Maurice Sendak's *Where the Wild Things Are* in which the wild things become larger and larger on the page as Max's temper tantrum grows in intensity. Sometimes the connection between text and illustration is suggestive rather than overt. In *The Tiger Who Came to Tea*, in one of the final illustrations a ginger cat whose colouring is remarkably similar to that of the tiger that had earlier taken the family's entire supply of food is trotting behind them as they return home after eating at a restaurant. This detail is clear enough to be picked up, small enough to be ignored. It has a whimsical relationship to the text it illustrates. In some picture books the visual matter actually subverts the meaning of the text. In Satoshi Kitamura's *Lily Takes a Walk*, Nicky, the dog who is, according to the text, supposed to protect his owner, Lily, is in a state of constant near-panic as he sees the menace in the world around them which she fails to see as she marches blithely ahead.

Any reading of *Lily Takes a Walk* requires developed theory of mind skills and the ability to hold conflicting information in the head in a way that is likely to defeat almost any pre-school child. It requires a good deal more of the reader than the superficially similar *Rosie's Walk*. It is a mistake to read sophistication into the responses of most pre-school children to illustrations. Jan Ormerod's retelling of the traditional story of Chicken Licken is enlivened by the visually told story going on at the bottom of the page where a baby has escaped its parents who are watching what appears to be a theatrical production of the tale. This is sophisticated illustration, but the fact that very young children are more likely to spot the baby than adult readers has less to do with any sophistication than with their limited ability to scan pictures and greater inclination to examine the detail rather than the overall effect. This is something that was spotted many years ago by Maria Montessori when she spoke of the readiness of children from the age of two to focus on what an adult might see as minor details in a picture. Her observation has been confirmed since in laboratory experiment (Montessori, 1936).

The criteria for judging stories for children aged two to six

Stories for children in the period when narrative competence is first developed (usually from three to six, rarely lower in age than two to five) should be judged by different criteria from those intended for older children. I am not suggesting that they be judged by lower standards, but that the standards should be different.

It is widely understood that children benefit early on from books that are little more than 'heaps', to use Applebee's term. It is usual to seek some educational advantage by making the overall subject of a heap a category of some kind (colours, animals, everyday household objects). This deserves more critical examination in the light of the evidence that greater emphasis is placed on the early teaching of categories in Anglo-Saxon than in some other cultures. There could be advantages to other ways of organizing books of pictures for young children. The main advantage of such early books is that they introduce books as a special kind of object, one that the child can share with a close adult. The content may be almost peripheral. Because you can only look at a book one page at a time, books introduce the idea of sequence by their very nature and thus move immediately from the first to the second of Applebee's stages of narration.

The books a child first encounters are likely to use isolated nouns in order to encourage children to use them. Once there is any kind of sentence, narrative begins to emerge. At this stage sequence and routine are the aspects with which children can cope most easily.

The early 'chain' will have the merest hint of narration about it. A good example is the 'touchy-feel' set of books published by Usborne in which one thing after another is identified as being someone else's kitten, truck, dinosaur or whatever by its feel, culminating in the location of the one that is 'mine'. There is a kind of narrative in these books in the search for the thing that belongs to the story-teller, and the chain has some logic to it, since each picture will depict a kitten, truck or dinosaur that is not the right one (thus underlining the possibility of similarity and difference combined, a crucial issue in the child's attempt to construct a picture of the world).

The easiest truly narrative sequence for the child to understand is one based on a daily routine because of the importance of that type of sequence in the child's growing understanding of the world. At three years old one of my own children was devoted to a book produced early in the twentieth century by Phoebe and Selby Worthington about a typical day in the life of Teddy Bear Coalman. The book is now out of print, presumably because coal fires and horse-drawn carts are considered too much things of the past to interest a contemporary child. In my daughter's case at least, the unfamiliar background did nothing to detract from the satisfying description of the coalman's day. Children of two or three have little need for climactic moments, and 'surprise' endings will probably not register with them. The implicit statement 'This is the way things are done' provides the young child with a satisfying basis to any story but one that will not last to a later stage.

Traditional tales whose narrative is structured around Olrik's law of three probably give many children in our culture their first encounter with the potential interest of a sequence that leads to a climax rather than constituting a routine. It is because this advance is potentially problematic that the telling of these stories always entails extensive use of repetition, with the same formula, often one that can be chanted or shouted, being used on each of the three occasions.

More complex sequences can be found in traditional tales where a succession of events leads to a climax in which an original problem is resolved. Chicken Licken discovers the sky is not falling. The old woman gets her pig over the stile by a particularly convoluted route. The old woman who swallows a fly overreaches herself in her desperate search for a solution. The basic pattern may be simple, but the need to remember a long chain of events can impose a degree of strain on the young child, especially as such stories can entail no more than a limited amount of repetition of phrasing. It is no coincidence that, while they have remained in the canon, they have a minor place.

A different approach to the creation of climax can be seen at work in one of the most popular picture story books of recent years, Eric Carle's *The Very Hungry Caterpillar*. Its success rests in part on the gentle way it introduces the possibility of disturbance in the course of a sequence and the resulting climax. The caterpillar eats an increasing number of goodies, first an apple, then two pears, then three plums, and so on. The rule for a sequence is established, one which rests in part on the child's appreciation of number. Carle then interrupts the sequence drastically by having the caterpillar eat one each of a number of things that give him tummy ache. Children of three can recognize greed and the chaos it can cause. Their hilarity at this turn of events enables them to get over its potential to puzzle or disturb. Carle then complicates things further by creating a new and happier climax as the caterpillar becomes a butterfly. The shape of the story is reinforced by the illustration (including the use of real holes in the things the caterpillar has eaten), finishing with the butterfly, which fills the whole page with colour. The book more than deserves its success. It provides a narrative structure that is just within the grasp of the age group for which it was intended and at the same time strengthens the child's newly developing competence at narrative. Attractive illustration can sometimes persuade adults to buy picture books that are not entirely suitable for the children for whom they are purchased. Carle's book seems to have established itself through its popularity among children themselves.

Jill Tomlinson's *The Owl Who Was Afraid of the Dark* is based on what is essentially a simple sequence, but one that requires a grasp of the possibility of different points of view. Thus, in spite of the simplicity of its sequence, it makes real demands on the child's theory of mind and capacity to remember a large amount of material. In its first publication it was illustrated with line drawings and later a more elaborate picture book version was produced, but it is essentially a story where text is everything. It tells of several encounters that a young owl who is afraid of the dark has with human beings who are not afraid and tell him that dark is exciting, kind, fun, necessary, fascinating, wonderful and beautiful until he loses his fear of it. The complexity of the information on personal standpoints renders essential the simplicity of the narrative structure, a series of similar events.

In some ways the most complex kind of sequence is the serial story. Television offers particular opportunities for the development of this form for young children. Since the 1950s with the original *Bill and Ben*, *Andy Pandy* and others, TV has had programmes in which a series of adventures befall an established group of personalities in each episode. The series *Bob the Builder* has gone further, linking the individual stories not just to an established situation, but also to a continuing story. The child viewer is introduced to an idea of longer passages of time entailing change and development rather than repeated routine.

Sequence and repetition go hand in hand. The wolf addresses the same entreaties and threats to each of the little pigs in turn. In *We're Going on a Bear Hunt* the series of similar adventures (later repeated in reverse order) is highlighted by repetition of the family's chant about not being scared of bears.

In various ways, therefore, repetition fixes aspects of the narrative in the child's mind and, therefore, assists the understanding. That is one reason why small children will often demand that the same story be read over and over again and will insist on absolute adherence to the text, something that Freud (1955) was one of the first to record. The more potentially disturbing the content (with threats and changes of various kinds), the more insistence there is likely to be on the precisely repeated text.

Television and video offer particular opportunities for the use of repetition. Pictures as well as words can be repeated with precision. The child watching a favourite story video yet again can discuss with an adult what is going to happen next and thus develop a feel for the narrative structure through interaction just as she can with constant rereadings of a favourite picture book. Our hunger for variety and novelty as adults can sometimes blind us to this.

The TV series *Balamory* has a structure built around a persistent pattern of recapitulation. Each episode opens with Miss Hooley, the local nursery teacher, asking 'What's the story in Balamory today?' Another of the central characters visits her with a task that needs to be completed and is sent by her to seek assistance from yet another person. These opening scenes are punctuated by songs that are essentially similar in each episode. Nearly half-way through the episode the character who asked for Miss Hooley's advice recounts what has happened so far in response to the question 'What's the story?' asked by the person to whom he or she has gone for help. The account that is given in words is accompanied by selected clips of the action being described. The episode then progresses to an inevitably happy outcome and Miss Hooley gives a summary of the story in Balamory for that day, again against a background of film of the events. There is plenty that is entertaining along the way, but the crucial element in the programme is the constantly repeated invitation to the child to understand and participate in the narration.

There are other TV programmes for children that emulate some of the recapitulation techniques used in *Balamory*, but they do so less successfully. For example, each episode of *The Fimbles* ends with a summary of the events of the day by Bessie the Bird, but there is not the same systematic invitation to participate in the narration. Stories for children of primary school age are unlikely to employ recapitulation in the heavily formatted way that characterizes *Balamory*, but it remains a crucial feature. Enid Blyton, whose success shows how much she understood about the minds of children, frequently reminds the reader what has happened so far in the stories she wrote for eight- or nine-year-olds.

The stories that are told in *Balamory* also entail something else – recognition that the person being told the story may not know it already. They tap into the child's developing theory of mind. TV and picture story books offer more opportunities for illustrating the possibility of false belief than mere text. In the picture book *Handa's Surprise* readers can see that Handa is losing her fruit to various animals, but she herself cannot. She intended to surprise her friend by bringing her fruit. She is herself surprised to see what is now in her basket, although it is just as welcome to her friend. Expectations can be falsified by events. The world is not governed entirely by routine. At the same time the cheerful illustration, the happy ending and the emphasis on fun and friendship make this threatening lesson acceptable.

Similar things happen in *Balamory*, where the central characters often risk upsetting others because of their failure to appreciate what is happening. Eventually this sort of thing culminates in the child's ability to appreciate the possibility not just of deception, but of self-deception. The five- or six-year-old who loves Hans Christian Andersen's 'The Emperor's New Clothes' demonstrates a sophisticated understanding of human psychology that has been generated in a remarkably short period of time.

The place of rubrics and conventions in stories for the pre-school child

Rubrics or conventions are important in traditional story-telling and in the case of children still struggling to achieve the basics of narrative competence. A possible starting point for learning the conventions that apply in our culture is learning what a book is and the idea of sequence in a book. A simple picture book designed for a baby may be the merest 'heap', but the child's carer will probably 'read' it from beginning to end, underlining a necessary discipline in narrative. I have seen a child who had not yet reached her first birthday look with puzzlement at an adult who was flicking through her favourite picture book from the back, take it from him, close it, carefully open it at the first page and 'read' it from beginning to end, then hand it back with an expression that clearly said 'Now see if you can do it properly'.

There are other conventions in common use that mark out stories as stories. One is the use of formal openings and closures. The children whose stories Fox (1993) recorded usually announced that a story was about to begin in some form of words or other. Lewis Carroll was in the habit of asking one young child he knew to tell him a story every day. He would always ask her to begin 'Once upon a time', saying that the story would otherwise be no good and the formula was most important (Bowman, 1972). Carroll seems to have intended this as a pedagogical device. Graham (1998) found that children aged six found it easier to retell stories when it was suggested they began 'Once upon a time'. Carroll's own stories for children never begin in this way. For that matter the great majority of children's classics do not do so. Collodi starts *Pinocchio* with this phrase, but only to make a joke of it, explaining that his subject is not a king but a lump of wood. Hans Christian Andersen normally used the phrase to retell existing, traditional tales, but usually opened the stories that related to his own tortured failure to find love with the depiction of an unusual landscape or an immediate plunge into the action.

For young children the fact that children's stories often involve animals, animated machines, fantasy figures (such as princesses or witches) or people who are clearly cartoon figures (such as the famous Mr Men) is just as important as formal openings and endings. There are many reasons for this practice. They include the shamanistic origin of many traditional tales that have ended up in the nursery. However, the tradition of using non-human figures persists in stories recently invented. This is because the device emphasizes that the story is separate from the flow of time and every-day routine.

The use of the past tense is another convention. It was one of the three that Applebee used to determine the narrative competence of children. The use of the past tense seems to be taken by the child to mean that the story is fixed. When children play pretend games their discussion is always in the present or future tense ('I'll be the prince and you be the giant' or 'I know, pretend I'm . . .').

There are also conventions of character. Bettelheim (1976) spoke of the way that characters in fairy stories are one-dimensional, either good or bad. There is more complexity in the ways that personality is described even in simple picture story books today. The child who behaves in a selfish way but is sorry later and is forgiven is a familiar feature. One such child provides the usual plot line in the self-consciously moral TV series *Clifford the Big Red Dog*. It is notable that it is always the same child who behaves in that way in the series. The possibility of moral complexity is suggested, but this happens in a restricted manner. There are limits to ethical sophistication in stories for young children. Faced with a retelling of a traditional tale that attempts to portray, for example, the story of Red Riding Hood from the wolf's perspective, young children are likely to become puzzled or confused and think that two different wolves are being described, a good one and a bad (Cooper, 1995).

Once a child has grasped the narrative conventions of her own culture, it becomes possible to play with them. Sheer nonsense is acceptable because it does not fundamentally dispute the conventions. The humour lies in what is self-evidently silly. At the height of Evangelical gravity in children's litera-ture in Great Britain, one author wrote of Giant Snap-em Up who was so tall he had to climb up a ladder to comb his own hair. Parody comes more slowly than nonsense. Reversal of expectation is even more difficult for young children. Davies (1989) describes the bewilderment of some when confronted with modern stories that reverse the conventions: when the princess, for example, acts heroically and opts not to get married. She recognizes the strength of their bewilderment, but fails to understand its origin, seeing it as caused by the way that sexist attitudes are strongly entrenched rather than by the child's need for certainty and clarity in order to understand a story. There are now a number of picture book rewritings of traditional tales for children on the market. *The True Story of the Three Little Pigs* by Jon Scieszka is a dishonest attempt at self-defence by the wolf. *The Three Little Wolves and the Big Bad Pig* by Eugene Trivizas and Helen Oxenbury reverses in an anti-stereotypical way the assumptions behind the traditional tale. Books such as these are really for children who are older than the ones who enjoyed the traditional tale when it was first told to them. They mark a growing sophistication about point of view which is underlined by the child's ability to look back on her innocent reception of the original.

It is easy to underestimate the importance of conventions in children's stories. Fox (1993) found that the pre-school children in her study (admittedly an atypical group in some respects) had already learned to employ literary speech, such as the inversion of normal word order. Her evidence demonstrates in a striking way the extent to which narrative competence is bound up with narrative convention. This is of crucial importance when dealing with children from cultures whose conventions may differ from those of white British culture.

Conclusion

Young children's fiction is only just beginning to extricate itself from fiction for adults and find its own forms. In part this is because fiction for children is still heavily influenced by adult taste and often by the nostalgia of parents for stories they believe they remember from when they were the age of their children. It is also because much appreciation of children's fiction has been developed on the basis of judging it as literature or seeing the picture story book as a product of post-modernist aesthetics.

There may be something to be said for either of these approaches for children who have already achieved basic narrative competence. Things are more problematic in the case of fiction written for children who are still in the process of achieving it. The books and television programmes selected for comment in the latter part of this chapter have well-established reputations. Parents and practitioners have discovered how successful they are with pre-school children. Understanding why they are successful in terms of their capacity to assist children to develop narrative competence is what makes it possible to use them successfully and also to understand other aspects of the child's developing mind.

Chapter 5

Narrative as a means of understanding

Introduction

Memory is vital to the ability of animals to survive. It helps them respond to familiar situations appropriately. Human beings go further, remembering unique sequences of events and being aware of their capacity to do so. Our narrative ability makes us what we are. The ability to grapple with narrative structures is an essential feature of our minds and, therefore, of the cognitive development of the pre-school child.

The issue remains that all this might be concerned solely with the normal development of general consciousness, a subject important in its own right, but with little to say about the development of systematic thought. It might be argued that narrative is about something that could be called 'ordinary life'. Perhaps that kind of thing can be left in most cases to take care of itself, with therapeutic intervention available for the minority of occasions when things go wrong. When it comes to more refined intellectual skills narrative is at best a starting point, at worst irrelevant.

This is the case made by Moffett (1983). He sees a natural progression in discourse. We begin by thinking and talking about the present, then begin to speak about the past. On the basis of that we move on to discussion of what happens generally and this allows us to consider what might happen in the future. Young children who are at the early stage of that process find generalization and abstraction difficult. They must make narrative 'do' for everything. In time they learn better. Fragments of generalization and theory begin to make their way into the stories they tell and they gradually become capable of more theoretical thought. As they begin to speak about the world, they play at being historians. Later, with the growth of skill, they play at being scientists. The higher our level of education the more scientific, theoretical and generalized our discourse becomes, but the stages Moffett describes are ones he sees as being unavoidable. It is a picture of staged general cognitive development that owes something at least to Piaget.

Moffett's portrayal of cognitive development fits awkwardly with the one outlined in Chapter 2 where the establishment of ideas of routine (a kind of generalization, even though closely connected with the passage of time) was described as preceding the ability to construct memories of episodes. His perspective is, however, completely in line with an idea that has played a prominent role in the history of thought. This is the belief that truth is somehow intimately connected to eternity, that anything that happens in time must be at best a reflection of an everlasting truth that underpins it.

This idea is central to the philosophy of Plato, who has been probably the most dominant single influence in the history of Western thought. In the Middle Ages and beyond, theologians and church authorities sought to identify what had been taught as Christian dogma 'always and everywhere and by everyone'. It was only in the nineteenth century that the idea that church teaching might develop was cautiously adopted. At the end of the Middle Ages the most radical intellectual movements defined themselves as a return to what there had been beforehand. The Reformation was a return to earlier belief and organization. The intellectual life of the classical world was being reborn in the Renaissance. To some extent the search for unchanging truth must have been a response to the fact that change often took the catastrophic form of invasions, rebellions and natural disasters. In the middle of the sixteenth century with its social, intellectual, religious and political turbulence, many looked forward with the English poet Edmund Spenser to

> that same time when no more Change shall be
> But steadfast rest of all things, firmly stayed
> Upon the pillars of Eternity. . . .
> *(The Fairy Queen)*

In the last couple of centuries confidence has grown in the possibility of change leading to improvement. There is still ambivalence about this. If timelessness is seen as the guarantee of truth, then narrative can, as Moffett suggests, have no real place in serious thinking. It is at best the starting point for thought or a source of entertainment and relaxation.

Against this perspective there is that which sees narrative as positive because it reflects something other than reason – the exercise of imagination. Since the late eighteenth century various thinkers have argued for the romantic against the classical, the Dionysian against the Apollonian, feeling against logic. Few would go so far as to want to see logic overthrown by feeling. On the other hand, many fear that logic may overthrow feeling. The idea is often put forward that human consciousness is at its best when these two are in balance with each other, a balance that presupposes that they are quite separate in the first place. A place has to be found for feeling and imagination. This is what fictional stories help to create.

Moffett sees reason as emerging slowly from the inadequate description of experience in narrative form. Others pitch fictional narrative against objectivity, seeing it as the context in which imagination develops against the threatened domination of reason alone.

An alternative to both these approaches is provided in the work of Bruner (1986, 1990). He describes the attempt to make generalizations that apply in many circumstances as 'paradigmatic' thought. This is essential to our attempts to understand the world. However, narrative thought is also essential. He rejects an opposition between narrative and the paradigmatic that means that one supersedes the other or that, at best, they have to be kept in equilibrium. Narrative is the means we use to describe unique sequences of events, which cannot be reduced to mere instances of general rules. We have to combine large numbers of factors (and the rules that may be associated with them) to construct a picture of what has happened. We also have to try to understand what events mean to and for ourselves. This can be a private experience, but the tools we have for metarepresentation come from the society around us. Therefore our attempts to understand experience always have a cultural dimension. This does not mean that we are determined by our culture, for example by the idiosyncrasies of the language we speak. Simple determination of this kind does not occur because events often contradict the tentative rules we have formulated. It does mean that understanding is normally the product of shared thinking and when we seek to understand complex sequences of events then that thinking is normally going to take a narrative shape.

Bruner's approach has the merit of giving a place to narrative that recognizes its cognitive as well as its emotional dimension. It does not set up narrative as the realm of feelings and fantasy, in opposition to the paradigmatic. His ideas can be further amplified by consideration of what happens in the natural sciences (perhaps the epitome of paradigmatic thought) and in the writing of history, a type of narration which disclaims any element of fantasy.

The natural sciences and their narrative dimension

At first glance the natural sciences appear to deal with things in a way that excludes narration. The mathematician Laplace (1749–1827) claimed that if everything were known about the coordinates of the universe at a particular moment of time, then everything that had happened so far or would happen in the future could be deduced. Of course, he did not envisage that anyone would ever achieve this. He was using a kind of metaphor to describe the way he believed the universe to be. It was an approach that made the history of the universe or any part of it a mere observation of the operation of eternal laws. It was a way of thinking that came to predominate. As the social sciences began to develop towards the end of the nineteenth century, they yearned to achieve a status similar to that of physics. What were merely trends in society were often described as 'iron laws'.

Narration had no place in the picture of science that emerged between the time of Isaac Newton and the end of the eighteenth century. If the laws of physics always apply, if all that prevents absolutely accurate prediction is the lack of information, then what happens in time is a set of instances of the eternal. This runs up against the difficulty of excluding narrative from the natural sciences altogether. It is true that all reports on experiments are narratives, but they are narratives of a peculiar type. Science has its own history, but that history can be held to leave untouched the nature of the things that scientists have discovered. However, there are aspects of that history that raise questions about the total freedom of science from a narrative dimension.

In the sixteenth century Galileo's description of mechanics in terms of numbers rather than the eternal qualities described by classical philosophers opened up the possibility of describing change in the material universe precisely and, therefore, creating a place for narrative. Mathematics may be the most objective and 'time-free' of academic disciplines, but it is also the one that allows for the possibility of arriving at a point that could not be predicted in spite of the logic-bound nature of the steps taken on the route. The patterns that emerge from the application of simple rules in chaos theory and some of the recent work on machine learning are examples. Galileo is also the person who did most to persuade others that the earth was not the unmoving centre of the material universe. The conclusion he reached is now so familiar that it is difficult for us to appreciate the extent to which in his own time it was counter-intuitive and contrary to received opinion. By pushing those of his own era into accepting a perspective on the universe that was unnatural, Galileo took a major step towards clarifying the impact of personal point of view on our perceptions – a key element in narrative. In the late twentieth century this became a major issue among cosmologists. An intimate connection is now seen as existing between the way the universe is and the capacity of humankind to understand it. A universe that was radically different in its basic laws might not sustain intelligent life comparable to ours.

The perspective of humanity is inescapable in science even when the issue under discussion is the history of the entire universe or aspects of the history of our planet, such as geology, in which human beings are not involved. Science is inevitably a product of human thought, whereas the extent to which that thinking represents an insight into what Hawking (1995) called 'the mind of God' is an open question.

It took a while for this to become apparent. Time was at the periphery of Newton's thought. He simply took it for granted that time existed, along with, but separate from, space, as part of the framework within which the universal laws operated. His approach excluded narrative. The one exception he allowed was the possibility of divine intervention as God was not bound by the laws of physics. Since no one could know what God was thinking, this exception did not allow for any truly narrative dimension. Then, in the nineteenth century, two developments took place in the sciences which opened up the idea of a history of the universe.

One came out of attempts to improve understanding for purely practical reasons of the workings of the new machines of the industrial age. The Second Law of Thermodynamics described the process known as entropy and led to the prediction that the universe would end in an undifferentiated mass. This was the inevitable outcome of the post-Newtonian idea that the universe is a closed system.

The second development was the theory of evolution by natural selection. This was the classic example of explaining later events by earlier causes. Darwin was very clear that his great book *On the Origin of Species* was 'in very precise terms a narrative' and he was not ashamed of it. He had been in his early days an enthusiastic story-teller (Beer, 1983).

Darwin's story of the evolutionary past with the implications that could be drawn of a progressive future seemed to contradict the dismal prediction of entropy. Strictly speaking, it does not. The two processes operate on different time scales. However, much of the culture of nineteenth-century Europe can be described in terms of a tension between the visions generated by these two discoveries.

The question of the origin and destiny, therefore the story, of the universe came to play an increasingly central role in scientific debate in the twentieth century. The discoveries of Einstein and others threw into question the assumptions made by classical physicists about the existence of absolute space and time providing the framework within which the laws of the universe operated. Einstein himself remained sufficiently wedded to aspects of the classical model to look for universal laws and absolute predictability. He was dismayed by the uncertainty that quantum mechanics introduced into this picture. The question of time and the reality of 'time's arrow' became a matter of heated debate among scientists towards the end of the twentieth century. Prigogine (1980, 1996) insists on the fundamental reality of the direction of time and the possibility of a future that is not yet determined. Barbour (2000) argues equally strongly that time has no real direction and describes the universe as a continuous curve. Most physicists, like Davies (1995), admit uncertainty, although they express the hope that the puzzle will be resolved.

There has been speculation among physicists about particles travelling backwards in time. If true, this would suggest the possibility of time travel. However, if a human being were to travel backwards in time, that person would still experience what was available to perception in terms of a forward direction. Even if what was seen was like a film being shown in reverse, it would still be for that person an experience, however peculiar, of time moving forward. Most science fiction based on time travel assumes, of course, a simple move to a new point in history from which the time-traveller continues to move forward in time as usual. It is not just difficult, but impossible, for us to envisage either a total absence of change or experience in reverse time order. Speculation about what the universe might really be like may make new discoveries possible, but does not liberate us from this fundamental experience – that we live in history, in a dimension where time moves forward. We are creatures of narrative. Pivčević (1990) argues that there is an inextricable connection between change (the fundamental element of narrative) and individual selves.

This very brief overview of the ways in which the natural sciences have developed over the last 400 years serves to illustrate that science cannot be divorced from narrative. There is no simple opposition between the paradigmatic and narrative. Questions can also be asked about the role of long-term patterns in human history.

History

It is sometimes said that our civilization is one that is particularly open to the idea that human experience has a narrative dimension because the Christian religion that lies at its base is founded on what is asserted to have been a uniquely determining set of historical events. There is obviously at least some truth in this. When the first 'followers of the way' preached their 'good news' to the Jewish and pagan worlds, they spoke of recent events and of a salvation that would come any time. When the Second Coming was delayed, this led to closer attention being given to what had happened when God became a man. Later, as the structure of the Roman empire began to collapse, the first faltering attempts were made to understand what a prolonged post-incarnation period might mean. Once again the fifth-century bishop Augustine, whose influence in shaping ideas about individual consciousness were described in Chapter 1, was of decisive importance. His book *The City of God* is often credited with being the first attempt at a philosophy of history (Augustine, 1972). Much of the history of the Christian churches since then can be described in terms of an attempt to grapple with the historical dimension of the faith and settle whether it is based on events that are of crucial importance to universal history or can be taken as a myth depicting eternally valid truths about the human condition.

Even if Christian Europe was particularly receptive to the idea of history as a narrative, it was some time before this idea took root. For centuries history was seen as consisting of stories about prominent public persons who could be admired for their virtues or condemned for their vices. Any sense of the continuity of history was limited to pride in the chronicler's own family or region. As soon as people became interested in something more complex and everyday than heroic glory, there was a move to abandon historiography in favour of the novel (Ray, 1990). The freedom to invent meant that the novelist's narration could focus on subjective feeling as well as on public fact and could support the main thrust of what was being said by the invention of 'facts'.

This left history needing a new role. The turning point was provided in the eighteenth century by Edward Gibbon's great book *The Decline and Fall of the Roman Empire* (Gibbon, 1914). Gibbon spoke of the virtues and vices of individuals, but his primary concern was the impact on the society he admired of barbarism and religion. This was also an ethical stance. In his case, however, the subject matter was wider than the moral character of a prominent personality and entailed an attempt to see a pattern in what had happened over several centuries. It thus opened up the way for alternative analyses of European history.

In the nineteenth century there were several efforts to describe an overall pattern to history and to discover the basic determinants. Marx's idea that all human history was fundamentally determined by economic factors is the best known. There were others, including the idea that history was to be seen as a struggle between racial groups, that physical geography was the primary determinant or that all civilizations underwent essentially the same process of birth, development and decline.

Towards the end of the century fewer attempts were made to find a single underlying pattern and more attention was paid to the question of whether historical investigation actually told us anything at all. Could we really know what had happened in the past? Most historians (inevitably, perhaps) answered that we could, that history was about the study of reality rather than a branch of literature. Von Ranke, who wanted to detach history entirely from matters of morality and values, said that the task of the historian was to describe 'how it actually happened'. This sounds very reasonable, but leaves open the choice of how to select the material of a narration from what 'actually happened'. Perhaps it is best to illustrate this with a fictitious example since any real historical ones will come encumbered with an existing body of controversy.

> Let's suppose that one morning the Crown Prince of Ruritania awoke, dismissed the servant girl with whom he had spent the night, complained of severe stomach pains, nevertheless ate an enormous breakfast, put on his favourite blue clothes, went to meet his Council of State and persuaded them that Ruritania should declare war on the neighbouring principality.

A political historian would probably select the last act as the significant one. Alternatively, he might wish to ascribe what turned out to be a very foolish decision to the Crown Prince's ill-health or self-indulgence. A Marxist might dismiss all the facts that have been outlined as peripheral and see the roots of war in the instability caused by economic development in Central Europe. Another historian might despair of finding the causes of the war and focus on the culture of Ruritania, pointing out the iconic significance of the colour blue in courtly dress. Even a historian who was especially interested in the personality of the Crown Prince would probably see little significance in the fact (if it was known) that His Highness had started to button up his blue jacket at the top and not the bottom.

In other words, history must be more than a matter of what happened. Too much happened at any moment of history for total narration of it to be possible. Some criteria must be used to select the facts to be recounted. At the same time, the writing of history must entail more than the selection of episodes that illustrate and extend the theories of social science, as Carr (1962) in an influential essay implied its role should be. There is too much that is accidental in historical reality. It is difficult to believe that history would not have been different had the Catholic Queen Mary had a healthy male heir or had Adolf Hitler died (as he nearly did) soon after birth. The Reformation might still have made progress in sixteenth-century England. Germany might still have fallen into the grasp of a nationalistic, charismatic leader in the 1930s. Even so, the detail of what happened would have been different and minor details can be significant in the longer run.

What has already happened is the material of history. It cannot be evaded. That is why the categories used in the two disciplines differ in their degree of precision. The physicist talks of particles and multiple dimensions and other things we do not encounter directly in everyday life. The historian also talks about things it is not possible to see directly – the Renaissance, the Industrial Revolution, the idea of democracy, the French nation, the middle classes. However, these are not abstractions in the same sense as the concepts of physicists are. The scientist attempts to eliminate detail to construct models that illustrate how the world operates. Concepts, such as the Industrial Revolution, are constructed from a mass of detail. If an entity conceived by scientists, such as phlogiston or miasma or universal ether, is found to be out of step with what is observed, it is abandoned. If problematic aspects of the way the Industrial Revolution has been conceived by historians begin to emerge, the term will probably remain but the description will alter. The relationship between the researcher and the material is also different. If a physicist speaks about the movement of the planets, the description may or may not be accurate, but in either case it will not affect the way the planets move. When a historian or social scientist speaks about the way that human beings have behaved, it will not alter the past, but other human beings will read those accounts and they may well modify their own behaviour accordingly. The future will change even if the past does not. The book written by the historian becomes itself a historical event that affects, in however minor a way, the rest of history.

This does not make history purely subjective nor is the sequence of events in history purely random. Past events have had causes and it is often possible to identify them. History can help us to explain how we got where we are.

It cannot offer precise predictions of where we are going, partly because those predictions may themselves alter that outcome. Politicians who refer to the 'lessons of history' usually get the present badly wrong. Our inability to predict the social future accurately is a source of freedom and responsibility, not a failure. The study of history offers us the opportunity to see that where we are is not radically permanent. It gives us a sense of who we are, situating ourselves in a narrative and providing some of the basis for future action. The explanations that historians offer (like the explanations we offer each other in conversation for what is happening around us) may be wrong, but they are not inevitably arbitrary or unreasonable.

Escaping the dominant present

Human beings can escape the dominant present. In fact, they can hardly avoid doing so. Towards the end of the nineteenth century several poets and prophets spoke of the need to adopt the simplicity of animals, which live entirely in the present. However, when accident or illness prevents someone from escaping the dominant present, the clinical evidence is that the result is not happiness but crippling anxiety.

Other animals may respond to situations similar to those they have encountered in the past in ways that reflect that experience, but they have at best a limited capacity to represent experience in symbolic form that can be considered separately from any repetition of the experience. There are two key ways human beings do this. One is to create abstract models whose constituent parts can be described with precision. The models are separated out from history. Thus, although they are produced out of experience, they appear to be timeless. This is what scientists do for the most part. Alternatively, the idea of time passing can be retained, but aspects of a period of time will be selected for their significance and formed into a narrative. This is what fiction writers and historians do. Both of these activities entail abstraction. Each has its advantages. Both are needed. They are used by all of us every day when we try to understand why something has happened, whether in the physical or the social world.

The kind of model-making in which physicists engage, with its reliance on complex mathematics, is obviously different from everyday experience. Narrative (whether fictional or non-fictional) is less obviously so. We tend to confuse the narratives we have created around events with what actually happened. That is why there have always been ways of signalling that something is a story (whether factual or fiction). Many cultures have clear rules about the time of day at which stories can be told. All of them have formulas for the opening and closure of stories. Literary narrative in our culture has specific conventions attached to it about the use of the past tense and certain stylistic devices to make it clear to the audience that a story is being told. Fludernik (1996) is right when she says that we need a 'natural' narratology that identifies the ways in which narrative arises in everyday discussion. That would still leave us with the need for conventions and rubrics when stories begin to form.

Some people will be better narrators than others, just as some people will have a better understanding of current models of the physical universe than others. Narrative competence has to be carefully fostered during the Foundation Stage of education when the basis for it is being acquired by the young child.

The next chapter will pick out from the content of this book so far the elements of that competence and the ways in which it develops in the mind of the pre-school child.

Chapter 6

The nature of narrative competence

The story so far

The ability to put experience into narrative form is something that develops over time. We are born with it only in the sense that the potential is there and in the great majority of cases it will be realized. It is an achievement. Adults can provide an environment that creates opportunities for developing that competence or they can impede it. If they are to be supportive, it is important they understand what is happening.

So far this book has outlined the key areas of research that help us to understand what the child needs to do to achieve that competence:

- the nature of human memory, in particular, episodic memory
- the ways in which the capacity for structuring narrative develops in the young child
- the nature of narrative itself, the place of culturally determined conventions
- the ways in which stories specifically for children have gradually emerged from general story-telling
- the weakness of some existing ways of distinguishing between narrative and other forms of organized thought.

Using this material, we can begin to outline the ways in which narrative competence develops.

The growth of narrative competence

The ability to remember is present in the young child from birth, if not before. In many ways we appear to be 'hard-wired' to register experiences and construct a repertoire of responses to them. Even before language emerges, children engage in pretend play. Such play is more than an expression of desire for experiences not immediately available (as might be suggested by a child pretending to drink from an empty cup). It is a way of separating experience out from the immediate present and giving it form. The form is often incoherent because a significant element of exploration is present in all such play. The child who plays 'gone' is investigating the relationship between continuity and change, a subject that has baffled philosophers. Exploration may predominate in pretend play, but experience is being given a new and different shape in such explorations and in that sense they can be described as stories.

As the ability to understand and use language develops, the child attempts to comprehend events in terms of routines and rules, in an effort to understood and control her world. Realization of the limits of her ability to control and predict leads her to appreciate that she herself is an object in the worlds of other people as they are in hers. These discoveries open up a world that can be more frightening, but also more exciting.

For some narratologists the structure of any story consists of four basic elements:

- an initial situation in which a number of factors are in some kind of equilibrium
- a disturbance to that equilibrium
- resolution of the resulting problem
- a new state of equilibrium, one which is not necessarily similar to the first.

Such a structure is clearest in detective stories or other types of popular fiction where action predominates. There is a quiet English village. Someone is murdered. The detective uncovers the murderer. Everything gets back to normal.

Bruner has something similar to say, but from a psychological rather than a narratological standpoint. We expect what is customary. Stories arise because an incident offends against what he calls 'canonicality' – in everyday language, what usually happens. If the general rules that appear to have been broken are to be modified rather than ditched altogether, an explanation has to be constructed that will accommodate the deviation from the canon. Young children, whose physical vulnerability and limited understanding of the world create in them a particular craving for security, feel this need more urgently. In *Acts of Meaning* (1990) Bruner cites research by a colleague who discovered that pre-school children were baffled when asked to explain why someone had been happy at her own birthday party, but could invent an amazing number of narratives to explain why she might have cried in the same situation.

When the child first begins to acquire some mastery of her own native language, she tries to articulate concepts of routine in words. That for much of the time she is trying to understand for herself rather than to communicate with others is shown by the practice of monologue when left alone which many children adopt in their second year.

The struggle to appreciate the problematic aspects of reality – her lack of control, unpredictability, the existence of other minds – leads her to focus on the ways that sequences of events can be structured. These provide the basis for understanding within the flow of time. However, the narrative sequences she enjoys will at first be simple and routinized.

Her ability to understand stories with more complex plots depends on the speed with which she becomes familiar with relevant conventions, which are, of course, a kind of routine. Formal openings and closures, the use of repeated phrases, rhymes or songs, the simplification of perspective and the repeated use of the same characters in story series are all ways of establishing a degree of predictability that makes it easier for the three-year-old to begin to grasp the basics on which more problematic narrative structures can be built. Repetition and recapitulation make good stories for three- and four-year-olds in a way that they would not for adults or even older children. However, repetition works best when it has a clearly ritualistic aspect. Children are unlikely to be impressed by the kind of plodding, repetitive conversations in realistic settings that once characterized the books used in the early stages of literacy.

Many of the devices described indicate the constructional nature of narrative. This is further underlined by the presence of characters in the stories the child is told who are not people from the everyday world. Animals, fantasy figures such as the Mr Men or the Fimbles, even machines and household objects acting as human beings are features of the majority of stories for the pre-school child. This convention may at first seem surprising. It might be assumed that the child, attempting to understand the world around her, would find it easier to handle stories of ordinary people, like those she knows. Paley (1990) found that some of her staff were disturbed by the children's evident preference for non-realistic characters and situations, and wanted to push them in a different direction. The widespread use of non-human characters in stories for young children is something that needs explaining and the explanation seems to lie in the fact that this device makes it clearer to the child that what is being said is a made-up story rather than part of the continuing conversation with adults about the everyday world. It assists in the development of her narrative competence by separating the story from the everyday. Much later, as an adult, she may appreciate realism in the novels she reads or the films she sees, in part because she is quite clear that they are constructed narratives.

As the child's ability to handle narrative grows, she is likely to show greater interest in characters from fairy stories with their relatively complex patterns of behaviour. It is at four or five that children often begin to ask whether a particular story is true. They have grasped the essential differences between fiction and attempts to describe what has actually happened, although it may be some time before they learn what their own culture regards as factual.

Gaining in confidence, the child becomes better able to deal with unpredictability and the idea that narrative is connected with the arrow of time, that what happens is more than a repetition of routines, that stories can have points of climax. She will also grow in her ability to understand belief and motivation. The child who is given real opportunities to develop her narrative competence will by the age of five or thereabouts be able to cope with an appreciation of these things that may seem childlike to the adult accustomed to the world of literary fiction, but are still more complex than anything which she would have grasped a couple of years previously. Along with this goes an ability to contemplate duration, not just the period of a brief story, but the fact that she herself is situated in history. She will understand that she was once a baby herself, and will begin to see her parents and grandparents as people who have grown up and to have some idea of the passage of life ahead of her.

By the age of six most children will have begun to distinguish in practice between

- narrative as a form of explanation of unique sequences of events
- theories that explain what happens in a large number of similar situations
- fantasy in which deviation from the everyday is enjoyed as a way of exploring possibility

although she will not use such terms and is likely to have difficulty in describing those distinctions in language of her own. This achievement is not accomplished once and for all. Her understanding will be refined again and again over time as she encounters, first as an older child, then as an adult, a range of stories, ideas and experiences. Children of nine or ten will still tend to give their own stories a heavily sequenced form, may have difficulty in retelling stories because they are distracted by exciting detail, and are more comfortable with moral simplicities and characters who are either good or bad or (at a pinch) are bad but repent. It will be many years before the child begins to grasp the fact of duration in its entirety and comprehend the distances between the present and previous ages of human and non-human history, will no longer ask grandmother what it was like 'in the olden times when you were a baby and there were dinosaurs'.

The components of narrative competence

I have used the term 'narrative competence' so far without defining it precisely. As was said in the Introduction, the basic definition is simple. Narrative competence is the ability to understand and create stories. It is possible to present a more detailed description of what the term means in the light of the theoretical material in the previous five chapters. It is a description rather than a fully fledged model or theory that is on offer. It is clear that narrative competence is one among many aspects of cognition that develop over the whole period of childhood and beyond. What I have done in this book is to point to the fact that particular advances in this competence are made in the period from the second to the sixth birthday and more particularly in the third and fourth years, and to use research and discussion from a variety of academic fields to suggest how this happens and the significance of it.

There appear to be five main components of narrative competence:

- the ability to understand or construct a chronologically structured sequence of events
- the ability to understand the passing of time and its significance, to see it as more than routine or the repetition of cycles
- the ability to understand the causal connections at work in narrative sequences: that for much of the time events happen because earlier events have occurred
- the ability to see that any narrative must be told from a particular standpoint and that different characters in a story may well have different points of view on events as they unfold
- the ability to use the conventions that attach to narrative in a particular culture and to appreciate that such conventions are precisely conventions, so there may be different ones in other places and those in our own culture can be subverted in various ways to attain particular effects and understanding.

The first four might be seen as relating to individual psychology and the last to something different, to cultural influences. That would be a mistake. As Bruner and many other psychologists have said, the cognitive development of the individual cannot be separated from the cultural context. It requires that context to occur at all.

The description offered here is an initial one. There is room to take the concept further. Among the issues that could be addressed by research are:

- the extent to which there may be linguistic markers in the stages of developing narrative competence
- the extent to which stages in the development of that competence depend on broader cognitive maturation
- whether any light can be thrown on the relationship between narrative competence and overall cognitive development by the spectrum of autistic disorders
- the extent to which the phasing in the development of narrative competence is fixed

- to the extent that it is fixed, is it a causal sequence with an internal logic or does it depend on some other factor at work in the brain?

In this book the object has been not to develop such ideas, but to sketch out the basic nature of narrative competence and its development in order to consider implications for practice in early years settings, especially at the Foundation Stage.

The support that is needed for all five components to develop may come in a sense automatically since parents and even early years practitioners do not necessarily think of the things they do with children, including the sharing of stories, as the transmission of culture. One of the things about the famous pre-schools in Reggio Emilia that visitors from the United Kingdom and United States often find most striking is their heightened awareness of the processes of cultural transmission. Even then such visitors are likely to describe the phenomenon in terms of moral values rather than culture.

However, if most adults caring for children do teach narrative conventions without consciously thinking about it, this is not simply an automatic process. Reduced opportunities for communication with adults, including communication that is focused on the paradigmatic or on instructions, can damage this process of transmission. Ironically, the fact that we live in a society that has, on the whole, an optimistic attitude to change means that we take change for granted and tend to concentrate on other aspects of the world when we are seeking to assist learning in the early years. This in turn leads to a lack of focus on narrative. In those societies where change is seen as more threatening, the means of understanding it intellectually are more prominent and more valued. This is why stories whose origin lies in the oral narrative traditions of less technologically advanced societies often provide the best models for stories for children at the early stages of narrative competence.

It is possible to speak of narrative competence as an aspect of the child's ability to deal with the world and see it as a single entity in that sense. However, even though it is based on our biology, it does not have a straightforward biological correlate.

Narrative competence as cognitive and creative

The description of narrative competence offered here is one that emphasizes the broad cognitive skills involved. This is not the only possibility. Fox (1993), from whom the term is borrowed, was interested in the ability of pre-school children to absorb and use quite specific conventions in story construction. This is an important subject in its own right and her book demonstrates how far the ability of young children to get to grips with the conventions of narrative fiction may be underestimated. Hers was the first real exploration of this topic, although others before her, such as White

(1954), had observed the unusual phraseology which children as young as three might use when telling stories to themselves or their toys, phraseology that probably derived from the stories they had heard. It is important to note that Fox selected a very small number of children for her study on the basis of the large part that story-sharing played in their upbringing by their parents and their readiness to assume the role of story-teller. Moreover, the two oldest children in the group were the ones whose narrative competence in both her narrower sense and the wider one used here appeared much more highly developed than it was in the three younger children. Indeed, one of them, aged four years and nine months when the recordings began, had quite extraordinary powers of expression which overrode, if anything, the chronological aspects of her stories. Because of the differences in performance between the children she studied in terms of age and the fact that the five children Fox selected for study were already unusual, we have to be careful in employing her material as criteria for what is possible for pre-school children. Her book provides a warning not to underestimate children rather than being a guide to what can be expected. Overexpectation of performance can be as dangerous as underestimation.

It is also important to distinguish between mastery of language and exploration of it. The child who is trying to construct narratives (or any form of discourse other than the simplest) is engaged in an exploration of the potentialities of language. Children when they first become fluent will often come up with constructions and images that are striking because they are the product of concentrated effort. As we grow older we become accustomed to forms of expression. Our speech is littered with dead metaphors. Discourse is usually a matter of custom; it is only occasionally that we think more carefully about expression. Children have to do this all the time. That is why their speech is often so vivid. To say they have more imagination or are in touch with some primeval source of inspiration is to fail to see the specifically intellectual effort that lies behind what they say. Both the ability to construct logically coherent chronological accounts and the ability to express experience in original ways are the products of cognitive development. We need to value all the instances of their efforts to understand the world and to express their understanding of it rather than argue a priority for one or the other.

The question arises of what is to be valued. Engel (1995b) asks whether we should value the ability to construct clear, complete and logically coherent stories or place a higher value on excitement and the ability to evoke experience. She notes that it is the former that is more valued in the school system in the United States. It is not just in the school system that this valuation applies. Tannen (1980) found that Athenian Greeks, when asked to retell the story of a film they had seen, appeared to give importance to the competence of their narrational style, while Americans concentrated on accurate recall. It is too easy, however, to see things in terms of a simple choice.

The focus of this book is on the cognitive skills associated with narrative competence, since there appears to be some tendency to undervalue them in comparison with other cognitive skills. That problem is aggravated if the response is seen purely in terms of valuing the emotional content of story-telling.

Fostering narrative competence

Pre-school children will develop some level of narrative competence (in the absence of any condition that disables them in that respect). The question is whether this will be fostered or impeded by the adults who care for them. There are a number of elements that are important in planning for this aspect of the curriculum.

First of all and fundamentally, there must be sensitivity to this aspect of their development. The level of competence each individual child has reached must be recognized, and what may be beyond her, even with support, must be appreciated. This appreciation must be based on close observation and assessment of the individual child. The problem with any statement about child development that speaks of phases of development is that these will be seen as precise and pre-determined. This is what went seriously wrong in Jean Piaget's original work in Switzerland and even more so in its application by many educationists. Just as children start to walk at different ages, and even after they have learned, sometimes revert to crawling or shuffling, so children's acquisition of narrative competence will occur at different paces and they will not always perform at their current peak. It is possible to generalize about the average rate of the process or about factors such as the influence of siblings which may impact on the pace. It is still essential to see where any child is and to appreciate the needs of those who are significantly ahead of or behind the average.

That appreciation must be reflected in the narrative material that is made available to children. It must be appropriate. Above all, it must be there. The higher valuation that is often given to the paradigmatic can lead to inadequate use of stories as resources.

The narrative material made available must be emotionally relevant. It must recognize the fears that will occur to any child and not run away from material that might be seen as difficult. It must foster the widening sympathies of the child who is beginning to develop her own theory of mind. At the same time it must recognize the limitations to the child's ability to imagine things being other than as they are. The reversal of established storylines is unhelpful until the child's narrative competence has attained a secure basis.

Appreciation of the child's narrative competence must also include recognition of her need to develop a concept of what is stable, precisely so that she can tackle the change that narrative entails. It is important to use standard formats, adhere to any established texts and give children real opportunities to understand any given story rather than use it as a springboard for other types of activity.

The child's ability to cope with narrative must be fostered by conscious and informed effort. To a large extent both parents and early years practitioners do many of the right things without necessarily knowing why they are appropriate. At best, practitioners may reflect in the activities they plan for children a kind of craft mastery that comes from watching more experienced colleagues at work and remembering what has worked for themselves in the past. This is better than nothing, but a more theoretically informed practice will be better still in this as in all other respects.

Appreciation of the way the child's narrative competence is developing must be reflected in all aspects of the pre-school setting, not just in organized story sessions. It should influence any exchanges with the child involving her attempts to explain her experience. It should influence how practitioners discuss what is happening in the setting or may have happened to the children elsewhere.

The next three chapters deal with various aspects of practice in the setting.

Chapter 7

Presenting stories in settings

Introduction

There are two reasons for using the word 'presenting' rather than 'telling' in the title of this chapter. One is that the word covers a range of activities, including the reading of stories and dramatic presentation as well as story-telling. The second is that the word underlines the fact that a kind of performance is entailed in all of these.

The Curriculum Guidance for the Foundation Stage says that children who have completed the stage are expected to have learned a number of narrative skills. If they are to become competent narrators themselves, they need models. These are often lacking. In the 1970s a primary school in Madrid experimented successfully in setting up regular sessions where grandparents visited it to tell traditional stories they had received when young from their own grandparents (Traça, 1992). It is doubtful whether many grandparents in Madrid today would have those traditional skills. They would have been rare even in the 1970s in most parts of Britain. Parents and practitioners can feel awkward in the role of story-teller, judging themselves against more polished and professional performers. This is rather odd. Someone aware of the existence of great chefs is unlikely to feel inhibited about providing a child with food. In spite of this, many seem to give in to a lack of confidence when measuring their ability to tell stories against that of a prestigious actor or raconteur. Probably the explanation lies in the fact that food is easily seen as essential, whereas we are still uncertain about the importance of narrative.

Anecdotal evidence suggests that the practice of reading stories to young children last thing at night is in decline and that they are often left to fall asleep to sound cassettes or televisions. This is sad for the parents as well as the children. The care of a young child entails many tedious chores from which it is possible to gain pleasure only on the basis of satisfaction in completing the tasks efficiently or of affection for the child herself, but the sharing of stories with children is a source of positive enjoyment.

If it is true that an increasing number of parents are failing to engage in this, it is all the more important for pre-school settings to compensate for this lack. In spite of this, the practice of presenting stories can fail to reflect that need. In some settings a story is used as a mere hook to attract the interest of children and then as a launch pad to get on to the more serious stuff of recognizing script for what it is, strengthening basic mathematical skills, understanding aspects of animal life or whatever is in the plan for the day. A story may scarcely have begun before the story-teller drifts off into a discussion of the different colours on the page of the book being used. There is nothing wrong with using a story as a starting point in this way. Engel (2002, 2003a, 2003b) is among the authors who have offered interesting and detailed suggestions on how to do so. The difficulty comes when this is the only use made of a story. At worst the purpose of the story session can be to get the children settled down before the parents arrive to collect them, so that they will be pleased by the standard of behaviour and the staff can keep on the right side of the caretaker by tidying up before the close of a session.

Of course, much better practice exists. However, this seems to depend very often on the natural talent of a story-teller in the staff group, just as the readiness of a setting to make use of music can depend on the availability of someone able to play an instrument.

There will always be people who find it easier to adopt the role of story presenter than others, but the skills required can be identified and can be developed by practitioners whatever their natural talent. Recognition of the importance of this task is what counts.

Attention to the task should be informed by an understanding of the nature of narrative, of the ways in which narrative competence develops and of the level likely to have been achieved by children when they begin the Foundation Stage. Such understanding can be reached through experience. It is likely to be strengthened by an awareness of the ideas and research findings outlined in earlier chapters. In describing the thinking that lies behind good story presentation, this chapter and the two that follow make relatively little explicit reference to that material, which does, however, provide the justification for much of what is said. The importance of repetition and rhyme in stories for pre-school children can be noted from experience, but is better appreciated in the light of psychological research. Above all, the fact that narrative is (together with paradigmatic thinking) a way of bracketing off aspects of experience to understand them better lies behind many of the practical suggestions outlined here.

Why have a group story presentation session?

If a successful story session is to take place, in the first instance the reasons for setting it up, and how they relate to what is known about the narrative competence of the children involved, must be clear. A session without this basis will fail.

There are several possible reasons for presenting a story. Among them are the following:

- because a child has requested it
- because the story is to be used as part of a wider activity, such as the celebration of a festival
- because the session is planned to be the starting point for an activity related to one of the areas of learning
- because it can provide a stimulating experience that will stand in its own right and has a part to play in developing the narrative competence of the children taking part
- because it may help to create a moment of calm and reflection
- because storytimes provide a useful way of marking key points in the day and establishing a reassuring routine.

This is not an exclusive list. There may be other reasons, and clarity about them is important. The session should not happen merely because 'We always have a story about this time' and it is too much trouble to break with long-established practice.

If the session arises from a request, then it is likely to involve a single child or at most a couple of children. There are practical difficulties for most settings in freeing up staff to be available for such work, but the possibility should be there in however limited a fashion. To be asked by a young child to tell or read a story is to be paid a high compliment. It is an expression of trust. It demonstrates that the child has confidence in the adult as a safe person to take her out of the normal routine, not just in the sense that the setting's normal pattern of activity may be interrupted, but in the more significant sense that the story itself will take the child on an imaginative journey. Because it is an expression of a personal relationship, individual story-sharing must be mainly about interaction with the child. It is important to know something of why the child wants this to happen and of the significance of the book to the child if she has, as will usually be the case, chosen a particular book. Precisely because it is about response to an individual, it is difficult to outline rules for such a session. The guidance that follows will, therefore, be directed at sessions with groups of three or more children.

Creating a physical space for narration

All narrative entails the separation of selected material from the experienced present. It is important to adopt and use conventions that separate the narration off in some way from the normal flow of interaction. The selection of a physical space specifically for narrative is one aspect of this.

This was recognized by those in the United States who pioneered story-telling with young children, such as Anne Carroll Moore, who gave story-telling a place in the children's room of the new Pratt Institute Free Library in Brooklyn in 1896, or Sarah Cone Bryant, who published what was probably the first modern book on story-telling, *How to Tell Stories to Children*, in 1905. It is endorsed by more recent authors dealing with the subject, such as Baker and Greene (1987) and Medlicott (2001). Their preference has usually been for a fully enclosed space with few distractions, to facilitate greater concentration on the story-teller. Experienced story-tellers prefer the horseshoe rather than the circle arrangement for seating because this is the one that best facilitates eye contact with all the children.

The presentation of a story should be a self-evidently special event, one requiring the children's attention. Some of the conventions attached to the format of stories serve this purpose. This should be reinforced by the location in which story presentation takes place and efforts to ensure that distraction from the story is kept to a minimum. Assuring the physical comfort of the children is another way of facilitating concentration. Nevertheless, the point is sometimes made more strongly than is necessary, possibly because writers on the subject often envisage an audience of children over the age of five. Older children may see the session as another type of lesson but without the usual classroom arrangements, and so become disoriented. If much of their experience of narration comes from television, then the need to pay careful attention to the narrator will not be as deeply embedded. It is possible to drift in and out of attention to the television without upsetting the story presenter. It is also the case that professional story-tellers, such as those I have quoted, are used to dealing with larger groups of children (about twenty) than would normally be involved in a story session in an early years setting, and a larger group is more vulnerable to distraction. It remains important to ensure that nothing in the space selected is likely to cause distraction, whether coming from other people doing things such as tidying the premises, or sources of discomfort. It is also helpful to have a second practitioner in the group to deal with any child who cannot easily be engaged, first to draw her attention to the story and then to take her elsewhere if necessary.

Choosing the story and its form

Thought must be given to the text that will be used and its suitability for the children for whom the session is designed. The word 'text' in this context means any instrument used to tell a story, including not just words but gestures, invitations to participate in the telling, pictures and other props. Both the story and the means of narration should be selected in the light of what is known about the narrative competence of the children, stretching them but remaining within their capacity. This is especially important if the group includes children with identified special needs or children from a culture other than the numerically dominant one who may have different expectations about the reception of stories (may, for example, expect the story-teller to welcome comment and observations from the audience while the story is in progress). There is no need to stick to the classic picture story books that have achieved success over the last fifty years, but such success is usually an indicator that the author has addressed the needs of children in the age group and it is necessary to think carefully about how a relatively new or unknown book will be received. There is also the point that, if children are still establishing the basics of their own narrative competence, familiar stories will be helpful to them, whereas novelty will be more engaging for an older child. It is important for the story-teller to like the story herself. If she finds it boring or is worried about whether any of the content is inappropriate, her discomfort will communicate itself to the children even if, in the hands of another story presenter, they would have enjoyed it.

Parents should be asked about the stories their children have already encountered at home and should be told what has happened in the setting. Whether the new or the familiar is chosen will depend to some extent on the purpose identified for the session. One possibility is to have two stories at a single session – one that is very familiar and one that is likely to be new to all the children. The familiar story may serve to relax them, the less familiar to stimulate them, but it cannot be assumed that this will be the case. The familiar may create excitement and the new story may be too strange to generate much immediate response. A great deal will depend on whether the familiar story can be listened to quietly or demands active response (such as joining in with the chanting of repeated rhymes). One possibility is to have all the stories over a period of time linked in some way, for example by including the same characters. A true serial is likely to stretch the memory of pre-school children too severely, but an equivalent to a television series could be considered.

Established fiction is the obvious source of stories for presentation, but it is not the only one. The more confident presenter may invent her own stories or put into narrative form recent events in the setting itself or from elsewhere in the world of the children. If stories are taken from the lives of the children, they must be constructed as stories. There must be formal openings and closures. The number of characters must be limited. The emphasis must be on action rather than intentions. The sequence of actions must be small. If possible, the story should be formed around the law of three or some such rubric. In any case it should have a clear climax. The use of conventions makes the composition of narratives easier than might be imagined. If the story is taken from the lives of the children it will attract a particular interest and help them to see their own experiences as things that can be formulated and understood in narrative terms.

Performance skills

Presenting a story entails giving a performance. Someone who falters will lose the interest of the children. The presenter of the story could heighten awareness of the fact that she is performing by wearing some easily made or purchased object that denotes the story-presenting role, such as a hat or a cloak. A further advantage of these is that they can be used by children when they are acting as narrators to make it clear that they have now taken on that role. Story sacks and other props also underline the fact that narration is taking place.

The presenter should study the story beforehand, if possible learning by heart both the written text and anything that is intended to accompany it. Close familiarity with the story allows the presenter to engage with children more than would otherwise be possible with a group larger than two. Story-reading is a perfectly valid alternative to story-telling, but it will create too many distractions if the presenter is constantly turning to the text to check what to say or do next. Cue cards are hopeless. At least a book, if it is large enough and the illustrations simple enough, can be shown to the children in the group. Knowing the story intimately will also give the presenter a better idea of how to pace it and of the elements that need the greatest emphasis. She will be better prepared for any parts of the story where lines are repeated and the children can join in saying them. Encouraging participation requires direct eye contact. Someone reading from the page cannot be effective in getting the children to join in the narration. If the story presenter is looking directly at the children just before getting to the part where they have to start chanting, she can signal by facial expression or in other ways the invitation to them to take part.

The story presenter should leave herself free to move. She may be happy to tell a story quietly. She may want to underpin what she is saying by movement and gesture. If she elects to sit down rather than remain standing to narrate a story, she should still be able to undertake those movements, such as leaning forward, which will assist the performance.

A formal opening to each story is essential. Some experienced story presenters like to have a formal opening to the whole session (assuming that it will include more than one story, as tends to be the case when professional story-tellers visit a setting). Both Baker and Greene (1987) and Colwell (1980) suggest a ceremony of lighting a candle in a semi-darkened room. In television programmes for pre-school children the start of a story is often marked by a display of electronic visual magic as well as the ritual use of words. 'What's the story in Balamory' and 'Imagine, imagine, imagine a story' (used in *Storymakers*) are both accompanied by such displays. This is beyond the capacity of any normal setting, but the use of a formula is always a good idea. It is easy to invent one and establish the custom of its use in the setting.

After a ritual opening the presenter should explain what is going to happen. Reading out the title of a book is not much use. Injunctions to be quiet and settle down are worse. The less the narrative competence of the children, the more they will need some kind of navigation aid, such as 'This is a story about a little girl who decided to give her friend a nice surprise.' If the story deals with a foreign country or a culture that is other than the numerically dominant one in the setting, some further explanation may be necessary: 'She lives in the countryside in Africa.'

The story should be told (or read) in a clear, well-controlled voice and with a steady pace, unless the narrative demands some slowing down or speeding up for effect. A story-teller in a small room may not need as much control over her breathing as an opera singer, but she needs some; otherwise, she may find herself pausing for breath when the story demands an escalating pace. It is useful to try reciting the story aloud at home, whether alone or to any audience it is possible to gather. The ability to control pitch and pace will come to most people readily enough.

Gestures and facial expressions illustrate the message of any written or spoken text in the same way as pictures in a book. They should, however, be part of the story presentation, not an additional or alternative entertainment. Some dramatization is required to help keep the children engaged, but if the performance is too lively, it could end up seriously distracting them from the story itself. Rehearsal is as helpful with gestures and facial expressions as it is for the speaking voice.

It is a good idea for the story presenter to record herself on a sound cassette or camcorder. It will help her to evaluate how well she is doing in vocal and visual presentation. Staff development sessions can be used for members to tell each other stories and then comment on the effectiveness of the presentation. This requires mutual trust to work well, but with good facilitation by the manager or trainer present it can teach some useful lessons.

The story should close properly. Some may end with the traditional statement about people living happily ever after. Some written texts have strong endings that make it clear that the narration has closed. *The Tiger Who Came to Tea* and *The Very Hungry Caterpillar* are examples. If a verbal text does not have a clear, firm ending, it is worth asking whether it is appropriate. Perhaps it is not and should be rejected. Perhaps a picture story book is being used and the last picture makes good the weakness of the ending of the verbal text. If the story does not have a strong ending, but the reasons for selecting it seem valid on reflection, then a conclusion can be added. 'And that is the story of . . .' will suffice if nothing more inventive comes to mind.

There should be a pause after the end of a story. Children need time to absorb what it had to tell them. They need some kind of airlock between the world of the story and the world to which they are returning. It is a mistake to rush into the telling of a further story just because one has gone down well. Similarly, it is a mistake to rush into some other activity, such as tidying up or an activity related to one of the elements in the story. If the children want to leave, it is worth asking whether the session could have been managed better or whether they simply want to go off somewhere quiet for their own moment of pause and reflection.

Props

Traditional tellers of folktales did not use props apart from some musical accompaniment. Many professional story-tellers in the modern world take a rather purist stance on the use of props. Story-telling in early years settings can be enhanced by various materials, but their selection and the manner of their use require careful thought.

Picture story books are the most widely used prop and, perhaps, the obvious one. Because such books are often shared with children on a one-to-one basis or with a couple of children, it may seem an obvious move to show children in a larger group the pictures in a book. This is not necessarily the case. If the book is too small or the pictures are too detailed to be 'read' from a distance, the children will not get anything out of them or may interrupt the pace of the story to take a closer look. Some picture story books are available in larger format with illustrations that can be used to show to small groups of children. *Lima's Red Hot Chilli* is a good example. Apart from the physical difficulty young children may have in seeing the illustrations if they are in a group of three or more, they are easily distracted by the detail in illustration and will not necessarily have the capacity to integrate written text and illustration in the way the author intended. This does not matter a great deal when an adult is sharing a book with an individual child or possibly a couple of children. The pace of the reading can be adapted to their needs and does not have to be that of the narration. It can be varied to clarify things or discuss details that have caught the child's attention. When the practitioner is dealing with a group of even three children, the possibility of moving at a suitable pace becomes more problematic. The use of pictures in a book is one of the most difficult aspects of story-reading and another sound reason for rehearsal.

Story sacks offer another approach to the use of props. They were an invention of Neil Griffiths, who now operates an advisory service on a free-lance basis, but who developed the idea as part of a project of the Basic Skills Agency. There were similar ideas around beforehand, but Griffiths made the story sack a coherent and well-thought-out way of interweaving story-telling and the use of visual and other material. He himself is an excellent story-teller who can make imaginative use of such materials precisely because he can operate without them. Figures representing the main characters in a story, toy versions of objects that figure in it, a picture that offers a kind of map of the territory if the narrative is based on a journey can all be fetched out of the sack to enhance the narration.

The relationship between maps and narrative is interesting. Originally the most accurate European maps were narratives, explaining in precise detail what happened if a ship sailed from point to point on a coast. Maps that displayed large areas of the world, as opposed to coastlines, were comparatively rare until the seafaring discoveries of the sixteenth century and later. Where they were made, their design was usually symbolic rather than realistically representational, with Jerusalem often figuring as the centre of the world. We do not think of maps as narratives, but maps that, in effect, told stories were crucial to the understanding of the world that European seafaring nations were developing a few centuries ago. Many stories in which action predominates are based around journeys. Where this is the case it is possible to construct maps with lines representing roads or rivers and simple depictions of the places where key events in the story take place. The display of such a map behind the narrator can provide a constant reference point for keeping track of the events.

Large-scale illustrations, such as 'maps', can be used as a literal and figurative background. There is also an important place for the small objects that are produced from the sack at different points of the story. The business of reaching into the sack to fetch out the object that is to be used next is much more interesting than the business of turning round a book and pointing to the picture on the relevant page. It has the same excitement as opening a present and can add to the dramatic pacing of a story while the background picture or map can provide a frame for the narrative content.

Story sacks can be used to house materials that will be employed in the follow-up to stories. This makes sense, but it entails risks. It becomes too easy when constructing the sack to focus on the follow-up and fail to think with sufficient care about the way the visual material will assist in the telling of the story itself.

Objects can be especially useful in introducing children to aspects of other cultures. If the story involves a flying carpet, a rug from the Middle East (or at least one with an appropriate pattern) can be employed. The experience can appeal to all the senses, not just the visual. Exotic fruit, cooked foods specific to certain festivals and their associated stories, musical instruments or recordings of them and other things associated with other cultures can be touched, heard, eaten, smelled or encountered in whatever way is most appropriate. The notion that the story must be listened to attentively can lead to the conclusion that this sort of activity must follow it as a separate kind of exploration. It is true that interest in the material can be distracting if the narrative is not simple enough to be kept in mind by children who may find that difficult. However, there is no iron rule that the story comes first and the handling of material afterwards. If the story is sufficiently well structured and the materials or artefacts employed are not too varied, then a natural pause in the story can be used for this kind of encounter.

While the emphasis on text, which is very strong in our culture, leads many story-tellers to be wary of objects that can distract from it, a good story-teller will be able to use material that happens to be in the visual field to illustrate what is happening. This is one reason why the outside provides a suitable location for story-telling. 'The giant was as big as that building over there and used to eat trucks like that one for his tea' is the sort of extemporization that the confident story-teller should be able to manage.

Puppets are another kind of prop used with stories. They can vary from simple finger puppets, which can probably provide the easiest form of illustration, to the kind of detailed and complex puppets designed for use with young children by commercial companies such as Folkmanis Puppets. Their handling requires some skill even if they are simple to manipulate. It is important to distinguish between puppet shows where the illusion that the puppets are enacting the story is required and the use of puppets to illustrate a story where the teller will want to make her own role in handling the puppets clear.

One type of puppet used in a particular kind of story activity is the persona doll, a device for opening up issues relating to personal, emotional and social development with young children. They have been used primarily to raise issues of discrimination based on race, gender or disability. Usually about 30 inches tall, they have clear characteristics that identify the kind of children they represent. They are used not to illustrate stories, but to initiate them. The practitioner sitting with a doll on her knee introduces him or her to the children, giving the doll a name. She explains why she is speaking on behalf of the doll and is quite clear and explicit with the children that it is a pretend child. The practitioner explains the doll's situation, for example that other children will not play with her because of her skin colour or disability. She explains that the doll wants to ask for their help or advice in this situation. The issue is always kept as simple as possible. In real life a child may have more than one kind of difficulty, but a persona doll is introduced as having just one. Children are invited to comment and the task of the practitioner is to reflect back what the children are saying, ask leading questions and pick up particularly on the contributions by children who may be directly affected by the situation under discussion. As in all story-telling sessions, formal closure is needed. A good ending is for the practitioner to thank the children on the doll's behalf for their help.

Persona dolls have taken off in the United Kingdom, as they have in the United States, where they originated in the 1990s. Their success is due to the way they address key aspects of the child's development at the Foundation Stage. When children of that age make apparently discriminatory remarks the reaction is often too coloured by horror and distress to be help-ful. The idea of the child's mind as a blank slate or empty notebook waiting for the adults in her life to enter the information she will need leads to the assumption that the child that has made a discriminatory remark, has been subject to propaganda and to an extent has been corrupted by it. This, in turn, may suggest that a tension exists between the values of the setting and the values the child is learning at home. In these circumstances staff can be uncertain how to deal with their dual commitment to equality of opportunity on the one hand and respect for parents on the other. Of course, children will echo comments they have heard from adults, but the greatest factor in any tendency to stereotyping is that at the age of three or thereabouts they are desperately trying to make sense of the world and have a strong tendency to overgeneralize in several ways. Children under five are more likely to speak stereotypically than slightly older children because of this drive for comprehension, even though older children will have encountered a greater amount of discriminatory behaviour and dis-course. At three years of age stereotyping is not necessarily linked to any hostility to others, although of course it may be. Just as children will learn that not all four-legged animals are cats or dogs, so they can learn that not all nurses are ladies. If an adult's values lead her to respond in a harsh and critical manner to what is merely a category error on the part of the child, this will get in the way of the child learning to recognize the initial mistake. The use of persona dolls in group sessions encourages children to think through issues for themselves.

It also encourages their developing theory of mind. By inviting pre-school children to think about how the pretend child would feel, rather than making a bald statement that a certain type of behaviour or language is wrong, the practitioner can tap into the child's own growing appreciation of the feelings of others. This can help prevent the type of situation where the child learns nothing more than that some behaviour is appropriate at the setting and a different kind is appropriate at home. The training videos that have been produced of persona dolls in use show some impressive examples of children thinking about the situations on which they have been asked to reflect and making the transfer to the actual world. The stories told with the help of persona dolls may not be stories in the usual sense, but they do place issues in the kind of narrative context where the child is able to reach con-clusions of her own.

Drama

Stories are seldom presented in dramatic form in most early years settings. The reluctance to engage in an activity where the children are a mere audience rather than taking part in active work is reinforced by the practical difficulties that would be entailed.

There is a place for occasional use of television or video in the setting, not as a way of keeping the children quiet while they are waiting to be taken home or for some similar purpose, but as an activity in its own right. A short video of a story can be combined with the telling of it, helping children to begin to identify the notion of plot and the ways in which different media have different strengths in the aspects of a story that they depict. Traditional stories devised for oral telling are probably not the best choice here. Stories designed for video or TV may be better. The showing of such a video can be followed by a retelling of the story or by getting the children to reconstruct the story in small groups. The fact that a video can be seen on several occasions over a period means that different aspects of the way the story is narrated can be selected for focus at different sessions. Some of the recent literature on picture story books has demonstrated how sophisticated children of primary school age can be in their interpretation of that kind of visual material. The foundations for 'reading' televisual images can be laid in early years settings if children are invited to comment on what they see. A three- or four-year-old can recognize, for example, the use of colour in animated film to depict mood or personality features. They may lack the vocabulary to express their ideas clearly, but that is all the more reason for giving them the opportunity to do so with appropriate assistance.

Video and DVD technology make the use of film in settings relatively easy. This is less the case with dramatic presentation using puppets or actors. Even if the setting has one or more people attached to it who have the relevant skills, dramatic presentation will still be a major enterprise. It will always be a special occasion and may well involve going outside the setting. Two organizations that have done new and exciting work in this field are the Nutmeg Puppet Company and Language Alive!. Both of these work at a high level of professional competence that produces entrancing shows for children, but their work goes far beyond entertainment.

One of the recent activities of Nutmeg has been work with nurseries and schools in East Anglia to plan a thirty-minute puppet drama, *Apple Pip*, and take the show around local schools and other settings. The set for this production is essentially simple, consisting of a single apple tree and backdrop, but the set itself and the puppets are crafted with great skill. Children who participated seemed able to recall a surprising number of details as they re-enacted the scenes – evidence of the skill with which the story had been told. The children are encouraged to see the puppets and ask questions about how they work, in other words to develop their appreciation of the fact that what they see is a narration that results from constructive activity. There is also a picture book retelling the story of the play, creating the possibility of looking at what can be achieved with the same plot in two different media. A teachers' pack is available.

Birmingham's Language Alive! is a company providing theatre for children aged from three to eleven years. Its work designed for single classes is backed up by resource packs for teachers and other early years staff. In 2002 the company departed from its normal practice of touring schools to invite children aged three to five to the Birmingham Playhouse. This allowed much more freedom of action in the creation of the basic set, which was modelled in some respects on the sensory playrooms used by many settings. An outline of a play about a group of shipwrecked children was written, but the actors were allowed considerable scope to improvise and the children were given time for free play in the set with its imaginative re-creation of the sea, the coast on which they land and an emerald cave.

Experiences such as these are ones that it would be difficult for settings to organize, but they offer an alternative to the more conventional stage production, which can, in any case, be less meaningful to the younger child. There is obviously a possibility for developing similar projects across the United Kingdom through collaboration between professional services for young children and local theatre companies.

Special needs

However hard settings try to be inclusive for children with special needs, they can sometimes give up when it comes to storytime. Once again, this failure may be due to the idea that stories are not very important and, therefore, it will not matter too much if certain children miss out.

All the practical advice that normally applies to storytime applies more strongly when children have special needs. Greater thought needs to be given to the space and seating arrangements, so that the children can engage with the story presenter more directly. Similarly, the use of hats, cloaks or other insignia demonstrating that a story session has started will be helpful. Additional care is needed to ensure that the narrative is within the competence of the children. Participation in the telling of the story and by handling relevant materials during the story itself will help maintain focus, especially if some degree of hearing or sight impairment is an issue. Physical comfort is important to concentration, and additional thought may need to be given to it. Children with serious visual impairment may be helped by versions of picture story books produced by the Living Paintings Trust in their work with visually impaired people of all ages. The Trust's 'touch and sound packs' include raised images known as 'thermoforms', which the child can 'look' at by touch, audio descriptions of what is happening in the pictures and colour reproductions of the thermoforms that make it possible for the packs to be shared with other children.

Physical disabilities have no direct impact on the child's narrative competence, but may lead to difficulties in her communication with the adults in her life, with consequences for this aspect of development as for all other aspects. Different issues arise in the case of autistic disorders, where narrative competence appears to remain stuck to a greater or lesser extent at the stage of the average two-year-old child. This represents a more serious version of the difficulty that most children face when getting to grips with narrative, and the measures taken to support all the children in the development of narrative competence will be valuable here. At the very least, children who have been diagnosed as having or are regarded as possibly having symptoms of autism must be given the opportunity to take part in those aspects of stories that they can enjoy.

Children whose grasp of a narrative is clearly poor can still enjoy the chanting of repeated rhymes or the handling of materials used in the presentation of the story.

Culture

Because of the demands of the curriculum and pressure from organizations committed to multiculturalism, there are now a large number of books, both fiction and non-fiction, suitable as means of introducing children at Key Stages One and Two (ages 5–11) to cultures other than white British culture. There are fewer that are suitable for children at the Foundation Stage. The issues of mutual understanding (or misunderstanding) with which books for primary school children deal lend themselves less readily to the action-based storylines that are suitable for the pre-school child. It is rare now to find stories with objectionable or overtly stereotypical presentations of other races and cultures, but the lack of more positively helpful texts for the pre-school child remains a problem. In many ways the best books are those that depict familiar behaviour, but do so with illustrations showing children from other races or cultures. Again, *Lima's Red Hot Chilli* is a good example. One possibility is for settings to construct their own picture story books, ones that either relocate simple stories that may already exist in our culture or ones which are based on folktales known to the parents of children from minority communities who use the setting.

The issue of cultural diversity is one for all settings, including any where all the children are white British. If a setting has a number of children from several cultures, other issues arise. When children come from families where English is not normally spoken, there will be numerous issues that affect the child's entire participation in the life of the setting. Storytime can present special challenges. In particular, children may be used to a situation where attention is not paid to a single story told by a designated story-teller, but to one where any story leads to others and appreciation is shown by offering new stories, especially ones that confirm the lessons of the first story told. The manner of conducting sessions has to be sufficiently flexible to allow for this. There is also the issue that stories told in different households may be quite different. Expectations that children will be familiar with a particular story, whether a traditional folktale or a modern 'classic' such as *The Very Hungry Caterpillar*, may turn out to be unfounded. At the same time, a child's home may be rich in stories that are unknown to others at the setting and which could be introduced.

After the story is over

As was said earlier, the end of a story should be formally marked. A transition must be made from the marked-off world of the story to the everyday world. There is no reason to make the transfer quickly. The formal closure should always be followed by a pause, if only of a few seconds.

After such a pause one possibility is to ask the children to reflect on the story they have heard, reinforcing the notion of the story as a special form of discourse. They can be asked whether they liked the story and, if so, what it was that they liked. (Asking them 'why?' is probably going to puzzle them.) They may be invited to retell the story in a variety of ways. This leads on to the activity of constructing their own narratives, which is the subject of the next chapter.

The other possibility is to link the story to other activity. However, stories can also occur as part of a sequence of related activities and therefore come somewhere in the middle. If, for example, a week is being spent in the setting on the celebration of a festival, then traditional stories associated with it may be introduced at various points. Stories can even provide the culmination of a series of activities, so that children bring to the story the understanding about aspects of the world that is needed to make sense of the narrative. If aspects of the story that might be unfamiliar have already been addressed, then it is easier to get the children to concentrate on the structure of the story itself.

Parents

If stories are taken seriously, then parents will be informed and consulted on them as they are on other subjects. Settings should:

- explain what stories they are using in presentation sessions and why
- seek information on the stories that children have available at home (this may help to clarify otherwise obscure remarks made by children). This is especially important where children come from a different culture and may be exposed to quite different stories at home
- discuss with parents how books, television and other narrative media can be used
- engage parents in story presentation, as story-tellers themselves if they have the confidence and talent, as sources of information about new stories that could be used, as people working on story sacks or similar story-related collections of material.

Conclusion

Good story presentation will always excite the interest of children and, as with everything else, they will want to try it themselves. This is the subject of the next chapter.

Chapter 8

Children as narrators

Introduction

The stories that are presented to children in a pre-school setting in the form of story-reading, story-telling or dramatic representation provide the essential models that they need to develop their own ability to narrate. Stories should be presented in ways that excite and engage them, remain within but serve to enhance their levels of competence and also make explicit the fact that stories are constructs. If this happens, much will be done to assist them to develop their understanding of the stories they encounter and begin to construct narratives for themselves. They need more than good models. They also need specific opportunities to examine narrative structures and to practise narrative construction for themselves. These will inevitably entail the active intervention and support of the practitioner. It will not just happen, especially in the cases of those children with special needs or with backgrounds (not necessarily the most deprived in other respects) in which there is little appreciation of the pleasure and intellectual stimulation children gain from stories.

There are many well-recorded examples of good practice in primary schools. Contributors to the book *Into the Enchanted Forest* (Brock, 1999) describe the ways in which staff at a primary school in Bradford supported children's dramatic role play. Another example is the use of 'story seeds' as part of the TASTE project in the south-east of England. 'Story seeds' are starting points for stories that are introduced to children by teachers or visiting story-tellers. The concept has been used successfully in history lessons as well as in relation to purely imaginative fiction.

Outside the United Kingdom, the Italian Gianni Rodari, an accomplished author of children's stories, produced in 1973 a book describing a number of story-producing games that could be employed by teachers or children. Rodari's subject is the business of constructing stories rather than their imaginative or emotional content, something that is still comparatively unusual. His ideas have been widely influential among primary school teachers throughout much of Europe, especially Southern Europe, although they remain largely unknown in the United Kingdom.

The examples just given all relate to children at Key Stage One or older. In primary schools story-making is often associated with the achievement of literacy and that has been significant in securing recognition of stories' value. (It has been more of an uphill struggle to achieve similar recognition of the potential of story-making at secondary level, precisely because of the assumption that most children will have achieved literacy at that stage.) Similar importance has not been ascribed to story-making in pre-school settings, in spite of the place the matter is given in the Curriculum Guidance for the Foundation Stage, which speaks of children making up their own stories, organizing sequences, clarifying events, retelling narratives, understanding the elements of stories and finding out about their personal histories and those of their families. Psychological research has demonstrated the extent to which basic concepts are established in the earliest years of life. The application of those lessons to the educational curriculum for children aged three or four has frequently created a concentration on such paradigmatic skills as the identification of categories, basic mathematical concepts and knowledge of the physical and social world. Narrative construction has been overshadowed. Where there has been encouragement of work related to narrative (especially in role play) this is sometimes seen in a purely therapeutic context, a legitimate but limited standpoint. Smith (1984) gives a critical account of some of the literature available at the time he was writing on the theme of adult-led fantasy play and its potential benefits to pre-school children from disadvantaged backgrounds. He has doubts (partly because of the methodological weaknesses of one of the major studies he describes) about the suggestion that such intervention can facilitate significant cognitive development, as demonstrated by improved memory and the capacity to produce longer and better-organized narratives. Both Smith himself and those whose work he summarizes appear to believe that such intervention is needed primarily by the deprived. Once again, it is assumed that narrative competence is something that will usually develop more or less of its own accord.

Imagination and pretence

Because the word 'stories' conjures up the idea of fiction, even of escape from reality into a fantasy world, it is often used in connection with those aspects of children's play that revolve around pretending. This is inaccurate. We need to distinguish between 'story' as imagination and 'story' as narrative construction. However, if pretending is not the same as story-making, it is a closely associated activity.

For a long time there was reluctance among developmental psychologists to acknowledge how soon in children's lives pretending becomes a central activity. All of the most recent evidence shows it emerging quite early in life, certainly before children are able to speak in more than single words or even any words at all. Pretence is the first kind of attempt made by the child to escape from the dominant present, to find a shape for things in a space that has been separated out from continuous experience. It is thus the foundation or precursor of narrative. However, it does not lead directly to the construction of narratives that can then have a continuing life. What is pretended may be repeated but it will not be preserved in the same way as a fully composed story. A narrative, once written, can have a life of its own. What is pretended still has a primarily exploratory aspect. This is always, of course, an aspect of narration. Authors do not always know how their novels will end when they begin them. Some appear to attach importance to having outlined a detailed plot synopsis before starting the actual writing of a book. At another extreme some modern novelists have played with the exploratory aspect of their art until it has come to dominate. James Joyce's *Finnegans Wake* is an obvious example. In either case some level of exploration appears to take place in the process of composition. In pretend play, this normally predominates.

It is a fundamental mistake to assume that pretend play is the acting out of a situation that the child already understands. It can be, of course, but the younger the child, the less likely it is to be so. Children use the activity of pretending to escape the dominant present in order to increase their understanding. The creation of narratives on the basis of this activity is something that may come later. Asking them what is happening and why it is happening while they are engaged in play and have not had the opportunity to absorb the experience can confuse them. The fact that what they are doing is exploratory allows adults a potential role in assisting them to conduct the exploration in safety and in harmony with each other. If it is to be useful, such guidance must be about creating the kind of circumstances in which the exploration can take place, not about imposing a framework in which the outcome is already given.

The best-known exposition of this kind of approach is that of Vivian Gussin Paley, an experienced practitioner in the United States who wrote up her developing approach in a series of books and articles. An early book, *Wally's Stories* (1981), gives a detailed account of story-making by children in her kindergarten. Even at that stage her emphasis was on the freedom to explore rather than on the creation of finished products. She speaks of a five-year-old using fantasy as 'a legitimate vehicle for thought' and of the way in which the stories produced by children were often outlines or 'stage directions' which were to be lived through as events rather than written up and read. Her later book, *The Boy Who Would Be a Helicopter* (1990), is another detailed account of what happened to a particular child over a period of time, but gives more detail on how the setting planned its work in this sphere.

The designation and use of physical space are central to Paley's approach. She identified a space within her kindergarten that was to be used for story activities. Within that space a further, smaller one was marked by tape as the stage on which stories were developed. This space was 'sacrosanct' when stories were being performed. Stories might run for a single session, but might just as easily run over a longer period of time with new developments at each session that could not have been predicted by anyone at the beginning. Only those children who were participating in the elaboration of a story could enter the space. Commentary by non-participants was welcomed, but permission of the group (or sometimes the single individual) constructing the story was required before a new character could be introduced. The stories were primarily about the relationships between the characters and often lacked any coherent action sequence. Negotiations were required at times to establish the nature of a character someone was being invited to bring into the story. To be a character was not to act a part written by someone else. It was to explore the potential of such a role. Because of this it could be risky. The boundaries between the story and relationships among the children in the setting were fuzzy. In spite of the creation of the separate space for story-making, the children had still not reached the point of telling stories that could be considered with detachment. One child was not prepared to be the wolf in a retelling of the story of the three little pigs unless he was allowed to run away at the end (unlike the wolf in the version with which the children were familiar). The exploratory aspect emerged strongly when children were inventing stories rather than re-enacting existing ones, even when the characters had been largely borrowed from film, television or other children's stories. The core of Paley's book concerns a child who described himself as a helicopter, a role that at first allowed him to circle round outside the social interaction of the other children, but which gradually became the basis for the others to welcome him into their own story-making activities. Although Paley set the framework within which the elaboration of stories became possible, she was concerned not to restrict the imagination of the children by allowing the staff to dictate what happened in the stories or insist (as some were inclined to do) on the stories having as their settings a more realistic or rational universe. She was also concerned to avoid imposing her own narrative structure on what the children had developed by using the material to diagnose their personal difficulties. She preferred to see any therapeutic function of the activity resting in the ways that children negotiated understandings with each other. Her caution and modesty, and her trust in the ability of the children to strive towards solutions, are salutary, given that in her own country most of the theorizing about children's imaginative play in the forty years or so after the Second World War was precisely based upon the usefulness of such material for psychodynamic diagnosis.

The importance she gave to the designation of a physical space is inter-esting. Brock and her colleagues (1999) also found it particularly helpful that they were able to make use of a designated space within the school they describe. Most settings do not have this opportunity, but there can also be a lack of imagination about the ways in which an appropriate space could be used. In written narrative fiction the book itself is the space within which the story unfolds and a reverence for books as objects is often found among children who are avid readers. However, it is interesting that many of the classic stories for older children are set in imagined land-scapes separate from the everyday world, such as Wonderland, Neverland, Narnia, Oz, the secret garden or the riverbank in *The Wind in the Willows*. It would seem that even older children need the idea of a special space. Once they have achieved some measure of independence of parents and other carers, they can usually find this outside home and school. When train-ing people to be childminders, I found that without exception they were able, when invited, to remember such a place from the time that they were eight or nine years old. Even younger children will identify such a space within the confines of the places where they spend their lives. This may not look very prepossessing to adults, as a key feature is that it provides some-where to get out of sight. A space under the stairs or the sink or in one of the less cultivated parts of the garden is likely to be selected. An imagined landscape can provide an alternative, but it will usually be a poor one if its source is the imagination of adults with all the fantasy ready-made. Pre-school children, having less autonomy, need the space that they have chosen to be approved by adults or, alternatively, need to have one desig-nated by them. Any rules on how it is to be used must give priority to their own imagination and ability to cooperate with each other. The designa-tion of a special space is a helpful, perhaps essential, objective related to the task of isolating key episodes from the flow of events so as to begin to construct them into stories.

Paley's original contribution was to create a form of practice that enabled children to conduct that exploration effectively and also to reflect on it so that the path into narrative itself was rendered easier. Her approach can be compared with that of Kitson (1994), who suggests a more direct and interventionist role for the practitioner in the development of fantasy play. He describes the ways in which the adult can nudge fantasy into forms of exploration that may not have occurred to the children themselves and sees this as important if the greatest amount of learning is to be derived from the experience. At the same time he is clear that it is the ideas of the children and not those of the adult that must shape the direction of the play. Essentially, he proposes that the adult should get involved in playing with the children as an equal participant, one who is, perhaps, more fully informed on what is being achieved, but who operates on something like an equal basis rather than directing the play and deliberately shaping the narrative. The adult acts as one of the participants in the drama and not as an author.

Inviting children to reflect on and explain stories

As children grow more competent in their understanding of narrative, it becomes possible to invite them to reflect on stories, either those that have emerged from their own imaginative play or ready-made stories from books or television or story-telling.

This can be difficult for them because it entails recognition that stories are not just there, but come from individual people. Some will be reluctant to accept that at first. It was the freedom that Paley gave to the children in her kindergarten to develop stories of their own that seems to have made them readier to accept the idea that stories are constructs and not simply given. In this she followed one of the most basic principles of Montessori, whose opposition to the use of certain types of story with pre-school children was based not on hostility to imagination, but on hostility to the various attempts of adults to impose their imaginings on children.

If they are invited to change or modify the stories they have heard, pre-school children will often struggle to accept their ability to do so. Their reluctance to see any deviation from a familiar text is mirrored in their hesitation about changes of this kind. They are most reluctant about changes in the personalities of central characters, to envisage that the wolf or wicked giant may have been misunderstood and be quite nice really. This is probably because at an early stage of their development of a theory of mind they tend to see character in terms of role within organized society rather than of complex personality. In their dealings with parents, grandparents and siblings, usually the first people they get to know well, the knowledge they acquire is of the roles these people have within the family structure rather than of their individual personalities. It is only later in life that they will begin to distinguish these two things.

Because they are inclined to see people in terms of their set roles, even children older than four are usually puzzled by the idea that the princess might rescue the prince from the dragon, proving herself at least as heroic as he is, until their narrative competence has reached the stage where they can look back on stories they once enjoyed with a sense of superiority and enjoy the disruption of their basic assumptions. Since physical characteristics are often used in conventional ways to depict the sort of character someone has, pre-school children will also be reluctant, though slightly less so, to accept major changes in appearance, may even describe such changes as 'naughty', presumably because they see them as a kind of lie. This reluctance to envisage changes in appearance creates a difficulty with illustrated versions of traditional tales. Pre-school children appear to find it easier to deal with suggested changes in the events that take place in a story than with changes to the basic characters. When invited to make changes, they often describe a complete return to the situation with which the story started rather than a climax that suggests a new interpretation of any one character's actual or potential behaviour. In such variations the wolf and all three little pigs may live happily ever after. This is something that can puzzle adults, since we are used to the idea that a causally connected and coherent set of events represents established fact, but are happy with the idea that moral evaluations of the individuals involved can be different. It is another example of children starting with a limited conception of event sequence and being dependent on the coherence of categories for stories to be intelligible. This subverts the idea that the paradigmatic always grows out of narrative, suggesting that on occasion it can happen the other way round.

Children may also have difficulties in analysing narratives because of their limited understanding of the situations involved. One of the advantages of Barthes and other narratologists, as opposed to some earlier literary critics, is that they speak of the work of interpretation the reader has to undertake and how often the text itself is only meaningful because of the assumptions that can be brought to it from other sources. Children who appear to have enjoyed a story may demonstrate that their comprehension of the sequence of events and more especially of any causal connections between them is surprisingly limited. Their pleasure may have to do with the liveliness of a performance, including text and illustration, or their recognition of a particular kind of incident (such as Eric Carle's caterpillar eating too much and getting a tummy ache). Their failure to understand may be concealed because the practitioner is eager to use the story as a starting point for something else. If the story is discussed and children are invited to retell it, misunderstandings may begin to emerge. This is a good reason for making the presentation of a story come at the end of a series of activities rather than as the starting point.

Collective story creation

Stories can be created by individuals or by means of a collaborative effort. Work on story production often takes place in groups in pre-school settings, partly for reasons to do with the difficulty entailed in spending a great deal of time in one-to-one contact with a child, partly because the group can appear to make progress through the suggestions made by children with greater competence or confidence. Both of these are proper reasons for operating in this way, but both of them risk leaving behind the child who has not followed what has been happening.

If group-produced stories really are finished narratives rather than episodes of exploratory, imaginative play, then they will depend on some form of scaffolding provided by the practitioner. It is clearly going to be easier to ask a group of children to tell a well-structured story with which they are already familiar, perhaps one whose basic narrative structure is determined by the law of three. Several approaches to this are available, all of them suffering from some disadvantages, especially if the production of something comes to be seen as the desirable outcome and attention is not paid to the extent to which narrative competence is being demonstrated or extended.

It is possible simply to ask children a series of questions that will lead them to tell a story they already know and to construct a text from this which is their own. The practitioner may say, for example, 'You know about Red Riding Hood. What did she do? Where was her grandmother's cottage? What happened on the way there?' This may help to reinforce the narrative in the children's minds, may help indicate their level of understanding and may lead to some original details being added to the story frame, but there will be no story construction as such.

A variation on this is to produce pictures or items that feature in the story (perhaps from a story sack) and ask the children to speak about them. A text can be created from their responses to questions based on the material and this can be seen as a retelling of the story, which they can claim as their own. This may well produce some interesting and imaginative suggestions from the children. However, it is likely that they will have difficulty moving between discussion about the pictures or material items and any narrative account of the action. The convention of use of the past tense may be observed when the children are talking about key episodes, but the characters and their possessions will be described in the present tense. Responses to the prompts may be interesting and the children may be happy with the book they have written together because it is, after all, a product, but the text may lack coherence as a narrative, a failing underlined by frequent change of tense.

A further alternative is for the practitioner to name a subject and ask each child in turn to come up with a statement about it, each contribution supposedly following on from the one before. Engel (1995b) describes an experiment with such a process in which the children, who were four or five years of age, failed to maintain the coherence of the narrative. Later contributors returned to aspects of the initial situation that interested them but that had been ignored by earlier contributors. The scaffolding that had been employed was too rigid to allow for any negotiation and agreement between the children so that real exploratory work was inhibited. At the same time it was inadequate to offer a real framework for narrative development itself. The tendency Engel describes for the children to return constantly to the starting point is perfectly understandable.

The difficulties with the examples given already arise from working with children in groups in order to produce texts. This is something that adults find difficult, so it is no surprise if pre-school children fail. An alternative is to invite the children to act out a story they have heard. Cooper (1993) describes the ways in which she has used dramatic re-creation of stories with pre-school children. She also speaks of the need for a designated space and suggests that both the children engaged in the re-enactment and any audience should be within it. She uses stories with which the children are familiar, reads or tells the story and asks children who have been given roles to act out the section she has just told. Action is prioritized and dialogue is kept to a minimum. The enactment can be supported by suggestions from the practitioner or any children in the audience as to how it should proceed. The object of the exercise is not to provide the audience with a dramatic performance, but to explore the narrative in an imaginative and playful manner. There is much that is owed to Paley here, a debt that Cooper acknowledges fully. However, Cooper's approach takes a further step. It underlines for the children the fact that roles in the story are simply that. It enables children to consider how it might feel to be someone else. This is different from taking on an existing ready-made role such as Barbie that may represent how the child actually feels or wants to feel about herself. It produces a further step towards recognizing narrative as a particular kind of discourse that is bracketed off from the general flow of events. At the same time it depends for its success on the extent to which the children have begun to develop a theory of mind that enables them to make that kind of imaginative leap.

It is also possible to ask children to construct a story and give them professional help in doing so. Children's theatre groups recognize the value of participation by their audiences. This can be taken a stage further: the children can be asked to design the story or make suggestions about elements in it. A particularly elaborate form of this kind of activity (and one which depended on external funding) is described by Gaunt (2003). Children at a school in south London worked with professional animators from 'D fie foe' to produce a short film about their own nursery that included both real-life and animated sequences. The school already undertook a good deal of work in which children produced their own stories and made use of illustration for this. The project, therefore, built upon existing work. The children chose the toys in the nursery that were to be brought to life in the animation sequences and provided the musical soundtrack as well as appearing in the real-life shots. The animation work was conducted in the school itself (something only made possible by recent computer technology), so that the children were able to see their suggestions brought to life quite quickly. The eight-minute film was later shown at a local cinema. The children had the excitement of contributing to a film in ways that were possible for them and benefited from learning something about how films, including animated ones, are made. This made it possible for them to see the narrative as a constructed product.

Children telling stories individually

Group story-telling is problematic. The various forms of scaffolding for the production of texts that were discussed in the last section all entail difficulties and are, perhaps, better employed as means of assessing the understanding of children than for the production of anything. Dramatic representation is another matter. It allows children to participate in the retelling of stories that are already familiar and thus explore the nature of narrative together as well as demystifying to some extent the process of producing narratives. It provides a useful bridge between the sort of attention to imaginative play described by Paley and the creative production of stories.

Given the difficulty that children at three or four will have in producing stories, or even reproducing ones with which they are familiar, there are considerable advantages to doing this with children on their own or at most in very small groups. The practical resource difficulties this would entail for most settings are evident, but there are benefits that should make the cost acceptable.

Because their competence will be limited, there are problems about asking children to tell their stories to a larger group. Story-telling is always a matter of performance and an adequate performance is not going to be secured from a child who has the structure of the narrative she is going to present less than clear in her own mind. In most cases (and certainly as a starting point with any one child) children should be asked to present their stories to a practitioner rather than to other children unless they seek that opportunity for themselves.

Inviting a child to tell a story is giving her an opportunity to demonstrate her ability in a particular type of performance and to explore her own understanding of narrative or of the issues with which her chosen story deals. It is also a significant opportunity for observation. In so far as this has been appreciated, it has often been in the context of identifying emotional or behavioural problems the child may have, whether these are major and deep-seated or the understandable reaction to something like the death of a family pet. This is a possible use, but one that has to be entered into carefully. Cox (1992) is cautious about the potential for using children's drawings as evidence of their emotional state or of the origin of behavioural difficulties, and the same reservations apply in the case of narrative. It is fatally easy to draw firm conclusions from material that is as likely to reflect the child's cognitive struggle with the task of constructing narrative as it is to reflect her personal circumstances. Interpretation is an inescapable consequence of reading or listening. At the same time, all interpretation must be tentative, especially when one is dealing with an author whose ability to shape her own ideas is likely to be less than that of most adults, let alone professional authors. It is the struggle of the child to construct a narrative that should be the principal object of observation.

The child's retelling of a story, even one familiar to her, may reveal surprising elements of misunderstanding. For example, one three-year-old's retelling of the story of the three little pigs has the mother telling her three children, 'Pigs! Pigs! You may come and go, but do not get eaten by what eats pigs!' In several ways, this brief extract suggests that the child has failed to grasp essential elements of the story in spite of her enthusiastic interest in it and its simplicity from an adult point of view. The pleasure in the story has probably been generated by her ability to follow it, reinforced by the use of both the law of three and repeated chants. That may have left considerable and hitherto unsuspected confusion about some of the detail. The last part of what the mother has to say may suggest that the child is struggling with the word 'wolf' (not one that crops up in conversation often these days, although it would have been more common when the traditional tale was first framed, and wolves occur as villains often enough in children's versions of traditional tales to be familiar). Of course, it may equally suggest a sophisticated understanding of the fact that mothers when issuing warnings to children have to tread a difficult line between drawing their attention to risks and frightening them. It is just as difficult to estimate the significance of some of the peculiar phrasing in the first part of the sentence. The mother pig's opening words – 'Pigs! Pigs!' – could be evidence that the child has failed to recognize that the relationship between the characters is one of mother and children. On the other hand, it could represent a recasting of her own mother's use of the invocation 'Children!' and demonstrate a real understanding. It is the use of the phrase 'come and go' that may be the most indicative. It suggests that the child has no real conception of the possibility of growing up and leaving home. She can conceive of a greater degree of freedom than she is normally allowed, that she should be permitted to go, but – even more importantly – should be allowed to come back again. The idea of growing up and becoming an autonomous adult may still be outside her conception of herself as an individual. As was said earlier, this is a realization that comes to young children with some difficulty and then only with explanations from a helpful adult.

This kind of thing points to one of the problematic aspects of using traditional tales with young children. On the one hand, the conventions of non-literate traditional story-telling can carry a story to a climax in a way the child finds satisfying. On the other hand, the material was originally produced for adults and makes assumptions about the world that may be beyond the perspectives of the pre-school child. This is a reason not to get too agitated about aspects of those stories that usually worry adults today – death, violence and the subordinate position of women – since these may not be as salient for the child as they are for the adult. However, it can be seen as a reason to invent new stories using some of the narrative conventions of the traditional folktale but based on aspects of life that are more familiar and to be grateful to those authors and illustrators who have produced so much work of this kind since the 1960s.

As well as failures of understanding about the world the story describes, observation may show up limitations to the child's narrative competence, especially when she is attempting to create an original story. The child's first original stories are likely to be disorganized chains or sequences in which a number of things happen, but the connections between them are at best individual links in the chain and the ending fails as a logical conse-quence of the opening part of the story. The need for satisfying routine still presses upon the child, so that a story that consists of a series of bizarre, unexplained episodes in which characters from television and mythology make their appearances and may engage in acts of extreme violence is quite likely to end with the statement that they all went home for tea. This can be puzzling for the adult listener when the child appears to be able to use competently some of the key conventions in story-telling, such as those identified by Applebee, and so has set up an expectation of a story with a clear and reasonable plot.

To speak of possible limitations on the narrative competence or general understanding of the pre-school child in relation to stories they definitely seem to have enjoyed is to risk limiting our expectations of them unneces-sarily. Often children who are able to read with some ease can become absorbed in works of fiction whose language and content are well beyond what they might have been expected to comprehend. This is a central theme in Spufford's book *The Child That Books Built* (2002). It is easy to overlook the fact that the same may be true of pre-school children hearing stories that appear to adults to be extremely simple. When telling stories themselves children may give entertaining performances long before achiev-ing mastery of the narrative form because they are using aspects of story-telling they have observed in adults. They may adopt standard phrases and mannerisms. They may rely on conventions to produce narrative structures rather than having to invent them themselves. In their struggles to express themselves they may demonstrate an originality that many adults would envy. In all these respects they can exhibit an apparent ability beyond what they have really achieved, but this is part of the business of establishing their confidence in the narrative task.

Fox (1993) has some stunning examples of this taken from a very small group of children including her own son when he was of pre-school age. The children on whom she based her book were in many ways exceptional. Rather than looking for a typical sample, she selected those who had access to stories at home, but she did not use material from children who had such access but were nervous about performing as narrators for her tape-recorder. Whether more children could achieve the same level of virtuosity if helped is an interesting question. Cox (1992) asks similar questions about drawing, pointing to the fact that in China young children are helped to acquire abilities in graphic art that we in Europe tend to assume are closed to them.

A number of things seem important if pre-school children are to display the kind of narrative competence Fox found in her small group.

- Children vary in the extent to which they are happy to take on the performance aspect of story-telling and their readiness to do so will probably depend on the availability of models. Fox found that the children in her group were quite consciously performing for her tape-recorder and some of them commented directly on this, while the children she decided not to use in her study found the presence of the machine inhibiting. The children also used a range of models available to them: not just their parents telling or reading them stories but also in one case a radio newsreader, some of the resulting 'stories' being imitation news stories told in the usual BBC manner.
- In order to enter into the narrator role, children need the formal acknowledgement of that role even if their audience is simply the practitioner or another child or perhaps a pretend child represented by a doll or some other toy. The use of hats, cloaks or other badges of story-telling office in the setting has the advantage that when the child narrator is allowed to wear or hold them it is clear that the role has been adopted.
- Similarly, props can be as helpful to child narrators as they are to adult story-tellers. Story sacks or similar devices should be available to children as well as staff. Their contents should be fairly simple and directed solely to the task of telling the story. It is also possible to find more direct equivalents to illustration. Pictures of single objects or people can be made available for display during the narration on a magnetic board. There are more and more ICT programmes coming on the market that enable children to create illustrations to accompany their stories as they tell them.
- Inventiveness in language must be fully accepted by the practitioner who is the initial audience, even when that inventiveness rests on what are technically errors. One of Fox's children produced a passage that is extraordinarily moving based on the use of the word 'weary' as a verb rather than an adjective, speaking of how she 'wearied'. It is easy to imagine someone losing the poetry, not to mention damaging the child's self-confidence, in her anxiety to correct the mistake in English, especially as the child's name suggests that she comes from a cultural background where English may not be the first language.
- Children must have extensive access to stories and thus models from which to work. Fox's group of children incorporated ideas from the

stories they had read and they used literary language such as inversion of normal word order as well as a number of other literary devices. If such extensive access is not available at home, then it must be created within the setting.

- The listening practitioner has to recognize that the stories that are told will still have much that is exploratory about them rather than being finished pieces of narrative art. This can be difficult if the child exhibits inventiveness in language. Hence props to inventiveness, such as repetition and rhyme, have to be applauded.
- Children have to be allowed both novelty and familiarity in the stories told to them. Repeated examination of favourite stories is as important as introduction to new experiences.

Children producing story books

Children can create stories not just as performers, but as authors and publishers of books. If they are to do this, they depend on being able to dictate verbal text and illustration. There have been reservations about this in the past. Some people are still worried that the exuberant spontaneity of live performance will be lost in the process of dictation to an adult. There is also the worry that too much control may be placed in the hands of the practitioner, and the children will become bored. 'Me do it!' is, after all, a common demand from the pre-school child.

A misconception underlies some of these reservations. The child may want to do 'it', but what exactly is it that she wants to do? This book which you are holding in your hands was written by me. I am the author. I did it. But, apart from any editorial advice, it has also ended up in your hands because of the work of a whole raft of people not concerned with the text itself, people with skills in such areas as layout, cover design, printing, marketing and distribution. Of course, I could have done all those things myself, but the fact that these tasks have been taken on by others has made the job of getting what I wanted to say across to people much easier. The practitioner who produces a proper-looking book from the dictation of the child is assisting in a similar way. Most pre-school children will settle easily into the role of the person in charge who dictates the verbal text and may also direct the nature of the illustration to be used. She is, therefore, helping the child to see her text as something valuable and comparable to the kind of printed book with which she is familiar. This is not just gratifying for the child. It helps to cement the idea of stories as products and of communication that can operate without face-to-face encounter. It can help the child develop her understanding of the idea of stories. It provides a model of literacy to which the child may begin to aspire.

Cooper (1993), whose ideas on dramatic representation of stories were outlined in the previous section, also offers guidance on the ways in which the practitioner should take dictation of a story. She suggests that this will normally be at the initiative of the practitioner and that this in itself will underline the significance of the activity for the child. She is insistent on the importance of good dictation practice, of frequent intervention to clarify that what the child says has been correctly understood, of checking that everything the child says is intended to be part of the story, of rereading what has been said so far to prompt attention to the task and of checking the whole text once the conclusion has been reached so that any changes can be made. She also speaks of the importance of offering encouraging comment throughout the process. Dictation in this context, Cooper says, is not about writing as such, but about what she calls the child's 'relationship to stories'.

The book produced by the child with the practitioner's technical assistance is an achievement. It assists her to see narrative as a form of construction, one of which she is capable, like the authors she recognizes from the world of printed books. This is why dictation of the simple kind that Cooper describes has advantages over the use of ICT. However, many children will gain pleasure from the greater professionalism of the product made possible by some of the software currently on the market and designed for use in pre-school settings. Dictation can still be taken by a practitioner who enters the text on to a template that has been produced for the purpose and uses the 'fill' tool to colour or modify picture templates provided. Software is also available that allows children to choose between alternative details in the narration of simple stories. This provides an excellent form of scaffold-ing that underlines the invention involved in stories while holding in place a structure that has narrative coherence. 'Branching story books', as they are sometimes called, are a good example of the idea of story grammars being adapted for use in the Foundation Stage and early parts of Key Stage One.

Conclusion

This chapter has dealt with the telling of fictional stories by children. Of course fictional narrations are not the only ones. In any conversation between adults anecdotes, jokes, descriptions of very recent events and other forms of narration have a significant place. The same is true for inter-action between adults and pre-school children. It is commonplace to ask them about things that have happened to them, whether in their lives outside the setting or in the activities of the setting itself. Sometimes this happens because of the practitioner's need to understand the child's background. Most of the time it is a practice into which staff fall without consciously thinking that they are facilitating the growth of the child's narrative competence. In various ways, in various cultures, the ability to tell stories is most often cultivated by the encouragement children are offered to recall what has happened in the real world. The next chapter considers the relevance of the concept of narrative competence to many aspects of the daily life of a setting.

Chapter 9

Narrative and real events

Introduction

Fiction is not the only type of narrative. Adults often engage children in discussion of recent events in their lives. However, because there appears to be a yawning gulf between the fantasy worlds of many children's stories and the everyday world in which they live, the connection may not be made between the stories that are described as such and the descriptions of events that emerge in the discussions they have with adults. The narrative dimension of many aspects of the child's discourse and their relevance to care responsibilities can be obscured. This chapter deals with that dimension, starting with the question of child protection.

Child protection

Disclosure by children themselves of possible abuse is closely linked to their level of narrative competence, but this has received comparatively little attention except in the very specific context of the reliability of young children as eyewitnesses in court proceedings. When a child says that something unacceptable has happened to her, the statement itself, whatever prompted it, especially if elaborated under questioning, will be an account of events. Her ability to make a statement effectively will, therefore, depend, among other things, on the level of narrative competence she has attained.

It is rare to find this fully appreciated. Once a child is able to form sentences, it tends to be assumed that there will be nothing problematic about her ability to describe accurately something that has happened to her, although her willingness to do so may be restricted by fear or some other emotional barrier. In much of the literature on child protection little is said about possible differences between three-year-olds and thirteen-year-olds in their ability to make factually accurate disclosures. If, therefore, the child claims to have been abused in some way, it is taken for granted that only two possibilities apply: either the abuse happened or the child is lying.

Many will be inclined to believe the child's disclosure because the alternative explanations for the statement she has made are in some ways more frightening than the possibility of abuse itself, suggesting not just malice, but an unexpected knowledge of sexual or violent behaviour. In the case of a pre-school day care unit in the United States several years ago parents fought vigorously to have allegations that had been made by children against members of staff followed up, using the slogan on the streets 'Believe the kids!' The same slogan was used a few years later in the Shieldfield Nursery case in the United Kingdom.

The slogan was a powerful one. It was also misleading. People were really being asked to believe in the interrogative capacity of the social workers and police officers who had interviewed the children. 'Believe in the professional expertise of social workers and the police!' is neither as crisp nor as persuasive a slogan as 'Believe the kids!' In Shieldfield, quite notoriously, readiness to believe statements in the form they had been taken from children led to injustice against members of staff.

A major part of the difficulty lies in the way that children may be questioned once concerns have been aroused. Two techniques widely used by police in interviewing child witnesses are intended to avoid implanting ideas in their minds. Cognitive interviewing, originally designed for use with adults, but used with children since the mid-1980s, is intended to prompt the witness into recall of details. All the available evidence that it is effective in the case of child witnesses relates to those aged eight or more. Witnesses are asked to be clear on the sequence of events and to consider how they may have appeared from the perspective of other participants. Both of these things may be beyond the narrative competence of a pre-school child. Step-wise interviewing is a technique invented for use with children. It begins with free recall and then goes on to questions of clarification about the details. An essential element of the technique is that the interviewer should not introduce any factor not already mentioned by the child. This technique was invented in the United States but has been widely used in the United Kingdom. There has been little rigorous analysis of its effectiveness, especially in the case of its use with very young children. Difficulties with both of these techniques and with more straightforward, less well-considered ones have led some to the conclusion that young children may lack the vocabulary to describe experiences or may be afraid of disapproval if they do so. These factors are judged to be particularly salient in cases of possible sexual abuse. Leading questions are, therefore, justified. This is problematic if it is assumed that such questioning will unearth memories of the sort an older child or adult might have formed. It rests on the naïve understanding of memories as recordings and fails to take into account the ways that memories are constructed in discussion.

We all help children to form narratives in conversation. A childminder, for example, may conduct a conversation with a three-year-old child in which she asks a series of questions designed to elicit a simple sequence narrative. 'Do you remember what we did yesterday? And who did we see there? That's right, it was the lady from your pre-school and what did you tell her?' and so on. This is a way of helping the child begin to construct the continuing narrative of her own life. The story that emerges is not the child's alone, but has been formulated partly by the scaffolding provided by the adult. It becomes an entity in its own right and, if the child retains a memory of these events, this memory of the story will be open to retrieval rather than a recollection of the events themselves. This is a way of facilitating the child's cognitive development into which most adults fall without necessarily doing so consciously, except in so far as they value exchange with the child. If one of the memories formed in that way is inaccurate (if the playgroup leader was met at the greengrocer's rather than the newsagent's, as the story has it), this will be for the most part insignificant.

Psychological literature is full of anecdotes about people acquiring false 'memories' that do not matter very much in this sort of way. Gopnick *et al.* (1999) describe experiments in which pre-school children are told where an object is to be found and then asked how they know it is there. The experimenter suggests three ways the child could have known – by seeing the object, by feeling it or by being told. There is a strong tendency for children to agree to the last suggestion that is made by the experimenter, whichever one it is. If that suggestion is that they might have seen the object, they become convinced they did see it. Howe *et al.* (2004) studied children in different age groups over five and found that vulnerability to false memories did not reduce with age and did not appear to be related to any traumatic experiences.

The power of adults to influence children well beyond the age of five is considerable and, as the experiments cited by Gopnick *et al.* demonstrate, can result from the way that questions are formulated without any conscious intention to deceive. It is the authority of the adult that gets in the way of the child's judgement. Sims (1999) summarizes some of the evidence on this kind of distortion. One study found that 42 per cent of the children interviewed as eyewitnesses in a sample had their responses modified by the interviewers when paraphrasing what they had just said; and when the children were invited to correct any inaccuracies, only about a third of them did so. In another study children who were told it was acceptable to resist adult prompting by answering honestly that they did not know the answer to a question about a recent experience were more likely to do so. Wood (1998) cites another experiment showing that in the case of ten-year-olds the readiness of adults to admit that they might not know the answer to something themselves encouraged the children to use their own judgement in assessing the number of objects in a set.

Such studies demonstrate that, even in the case of children older than five, distorted narratives can be created around real events, but it is possible to support children in resisting pressures of that kind. The pre-school child is much more vulnerable, since her ability to construct narratives herself is limited. It is quite natural for her to be dependent on a supportive adult to formulate the narrative that encapsulates her memory. Distortions can then easily arise because of the agenda the adult is following. The debate on child protection has been bedevilled by ideological persuasions of all kinds, so the chances of distortion of a child's recall are even greater than they would normally be. At one time the most common distortion would have been the suppression of possible evidence of abuse. Since the 1980s it has probably been to firm up such evidence. In either case it is a distortion. The child may also be frightened by the anxious response of a parent to a casually made comment and seize on the form of words that appears to bring the interrogation to an end (just as the same child might claim not to have broken something when she was seen doing so). The story that ends the interrogation, whether it is that abuse has taken place or that nothing at all has happened, may or may not be accurate. Once it is fixed as a narrative between parent and child, it may be impossible to shift it from the child's memory, let alone the parent's.

This is not to say that disclosures of abuse by young children should be dismissed or that it is impossible to get at the truth behind something they say. It is to argue that the interpretation of their words has to take into account their limited ability to frame narratives as well as factors that have more often been identified, such as the difficulty they may have in describing an abusive incident because of limited vocabulary or fear or shame. Where such difficulties become the grounds for leading questions the potential for distortion is considerable.

Some of the issues that arise can be illustrated by a fictitious example:

A three-year-old child is taken by her mother to the Accident and Emergency Unit of the local hospital with a large bruise on her forehead. The mother explains that the child fell and hit her head against a piece of furniture. The child seems happy and relaxed, so no immediate suspicions are aroused. The injury proves not to be serious.

The next day while she is at nursery one of the staff observing her injury says, 'Oh dear! Look at your poor head! What happened?' The child replies, 'Mummy threw the car.' A child protection investigation is launched because the child appears to have made an allegation that her mother had thrown a car (presumably a toy car) at her.

Two outcomes are possible.

In one scenario the child is asked to confirm that her mother threw something at her and, after some initial hesitation, she agrees, adding that her mother had been angry. Child protection measures are put in place. No further abuse occurs. The professionals congratulate themselves on the effectiveness of their intervention. The parents feel pretty bruised by the experience and the mother continues to assert her innocence.

In the other scenario more careful investigation produces a different account, which is finally accepted as the accurate one. The mother had arrived home with her daughter to find that her son had failed to tidy up his bedroom with his father after playing there while she was out. In a rare display of temper (brought on by the fact that the subject of tidying up had become a slightly fraught one in the family) she threw one of the larger toys across the room before starting the task of tidying up herself. The toy car ended up on the landing outside, where the three-year-old tripped over it, banging her head on a small storage unit on the landing.

The difficulty here started with the miscommunication between the nursery worker and the child. Although she would never have put the matter in such formal language, the nursery worker when asking 'What happened?' was saying in effect 'Describe to me the sequence of events which led to the injury you have sustained. Produce a clear, well-centred narrative in which the causal connections between events in the sequence are explicitly identified.' The child has probably interpreted what was said as 'Something unusual must have happened. What was it?' The most unusual thing that happened was that her mother engaged in a rare display of ill-temper. It was fascinating and exciting (if just a bit worrying) to know that her mother could have temper tantrums too. All this was much more worthy of attention than one of the frequent bumps and bruises in her life as a young child. On the other hand, she may have been struggling to compose a causally connected sequence of events and appreciated that the toy car was on the landing, where it was not usually to be found, because her mother had thrown it, but the reproduction of the sequence was beyond her ability.

Inaccuracies in disclosures are likely to be a matter of incompetence rather than of fantasy or lying. One of the fascinating aspects of the American case mentioned above is that many of the stories that the children told about their alleged abuse involved flying saucers and other apparently fantastic elements. The prosecution persuaded the courts that it was possible to distinguish what was fantasy from what was realistic in the children's stories. Fantastic elements, such as the flying saucers, could be discounted because they were obviously fantasy and we all know that children spend much of their time fantasizing. On the other hand, the stories of sexual abuse were possible, so either they were true or the children were lying. There was no reason to think they were lying or that, without having been victims of sexual abuse, they would have been able to describe some of the activities they did describe. The defence argued unsuccessfully in their response that the fantastic elements in the children's stories cast doubt on everything they had to say about the setting and its staff. Perhaps, being so young, they could not distinguish fact from fantasy. Eminent child development experts had said as much about all children of their age.

In fact, the evidence from psychological research is that children are capable, on the whole, of distinguishing between truth and lies, reality and fantasy, even at three and four. There are limits to this ability. Robinson (1997) found that the eight- and nine-year-olds she studied could understand the distinction between factual and fictional programmes on television, but were to some extent confused about where to place realist drama such as *Grange Hill* or some of the adult soaps they watched with their parents. Qin *et al.* (1997) cite the evidence of Annon that four-year-olds were no more likely than adults to confuse fact and fantasy, but added significantly that the material had to be well 'encoded' and that children could become confused if the event was complex. In other words, their ability to distinguish fact from fantasy was linked to their narrative competence and the extent to which adults had assisted them to construct an appropriate narrative.

The mysterious flying saucers may have been neither proof that the stories the children offered were based on fantasy nor an irrelevance that could be ignored. They are unlikely to have been introduced casually or arbitrarily. Perhaps from some of their television viewing the children had come to connect visiting aliens with sinister events. Flying saucers would then have been relevant to the narratives that emerged. They were the sort of thing you would expect to be involved if something nasty and unusual happened. In trying to describe events that were unusual and whose narration aroused powerful and negative feelings among trusted adults, the children may well have resorted to a kind of metaphor without having the literary ability to frame it adequately. After all, if an adult describing an unpleasant personal experience exclaims 'It was a nightmare!' listeners are unlikely to assume that this proves the speaker dreamed the episode rather than experienced it. The inept use of metaphors by children proves nothing in itself about the accuracy or inaccuracy of their accounts. It does indicate the extent to which their stories were constructs and more careful investigation at the time would have examined the process by which they were constructed. How much was suggested by the interviewers? To what extent did the children share their stories with each other? It is a pity that neither side in the forensic battle seems to have made any attempt to understand the role played by the fantastic elements in the way that the children encoded the events they were describing. Had there been better recognition of the narrative nature of disclosure, a clearer picture might have emerged of the reality behind the stories. The naïve assumption that memories are recordings got in the way, as it has too often.

The issue of narrative competence is relevant to the ways in which an abused child is treated as well as to the detection of abuse in the first instance. With adults and older children, the construction of satisfactory narratives provides a way of moving beyond the original trauma. Psychoanalysis can be characterized (over-simply) as a process for generating narratives about the patient's past that are satisfactory in so far as they enable the patient to live a more contented life. Freud himself was always aware of the narrative dimension of his approach. He believed his method could unearth the hidden past, but accepted that it could not predict the future of any one person accurately. Closure was something that happened, as in all narration, only in retrospect. Some therapists use the technique known as 'coherent narrative' to help clients in a similar way (White and Epston, 1990). Social workers supporting children whose lives have been marked by traumatic events have often worked with them on what are called life story books to help them give a more manageable shape to their trauma and place it in a more positive overall context (Rose and Philpot, 2004). Outside the field of psychotherapy medical personnel are learning the importance of encouraging patients to describe their conditions in narrative terms rather than as collections of symptoms (Launer, 2002). Approaches to therapy that rely to a greater or lesser extent on encouraging the patient or client to construct the problem in narrative terms build on the ways in which narrative assists us to conceptualize difficulties, bracketing them off from the flow of life so as to make them intelligible.

Most therapeutic techniques that entail the use of narrative construction take basic narrative competence for granted, even if they are sometimes predicated on the belief that trauma has damaged the ability of children to tell their stories freely. Narrative competence requires more than language: understanding this is the key element in working with children aged two to six (or thereabouts) on matters of child protection. It is one of the things that make really listening to children difficult, sometimes too difficult for the professionals involved. People like simple answers. Do we believe the children or not? Reality is more complicated.

Health and safety

The regulation of childminding and day care for pre-school children had its origin in a series of public scandals in the late 1940s about serious harm coming to children cared for outside their own homes or those of close family members. The concern to protect children from accidental harm, including infection, remains a major priority for both practitioners and childcare inspectors. Indeed, some have argued that in the United Kingdom the emphasis on safety is too one-sided, even hysterical. Against such accusations there are the inevitable counter-arguments that no one in their right mind would want a young child to suffer any injury, let alone a serious or fatal one, so that safety just has to remain a major concern.

In such disputes the role of the child herself can be forgotten. The controversy is usually conducted in terms of the need for the adult to provide as safe an environment as possible in the face of the child's problematic desire for freedom and adventure. There are no apparent ways of settling the difference apart from victory for one side or the other or, alternatively, an uneasy compromise. The route out of this dilemma lies in greater appreciation of what the child's narrative competence does or does not allow her to do in the way of protecting herself.

From a very young age babies show self-preservative caution in the face of immediate dangers, such as steep drops, heat or even things that may not necessarily signal danger, such as sudden loud noises. Children under two can be persuaded to brave such dangers if they are encouraged by a trusted adult, but they are alert to the presence of risk and, left to their own devices, will remain cautious. On the other hand, they do have a keen appreciation of their own abilities and of things they can now do that were beyond them only yesterday. They will, as a result, tackle climbs or other tasks that cause anxiety to their adult carers.

This is not mere fecklessness on the child's part. A two-year-old will tackle a climb or other task that looks risky to an adult because she can focus on each step at a time and is capable of assessing accurately her ability to manage each of those separate risks. What makes such play look dangerous is the adult's own ability to envisage what might go wrong, the ability to generate stories about a hypothetical future. The young child's focus is on the immediate task and not that kind of longer-term perspective.

This is only partly a matter of knowledge. Superior knowledge can be crucial. The adult will know that not all brightly coloured pills are sweets, that not all clear liquids are drinkable, but this will probably be outside the knowledge of a young child and her natural caution will not be triggered by things that look familiar and, therefore, safe but are in reality quite deadly. The obvious answer is to keep the medication and cleaning fluids well out of reach. On the other hand, knowledge is not everything. The adult's awareness of what can happen when there is a fall from a height may be more detailed than that of a two-year-old, but the child's knowledge will still be sufficient to persuade her that she does not want to fall. Where the adult differs is in her ability to envisage a series of causally linked events and, as a result, the potential ultimate outcome of a venture whose first steps feel quite safe. The adult will appreciate that standing on the edge of a chair to reach something can in turn lead to the chair overbalancing, which can in turn lead to a fall and thus to injury. The younger a child is, the more difficult she will find it to imagine that sequence. Her inability may lead her to make more realistic assessments of whether she can manage the next stage in the process of a climb (where the adult's imagination may go into overdrive), but it will not enable her to connect the initial steps with the possible final disaster. If she can get on the chair safely, that is all right. If she can reach for the sweets, that is all right. The fact that reaching for them can have a result additional to getting within gripping range of them may be outside the limited representation she can achieve of the total situation. The more complex the series of events leading from the initial move to possible disaster, the more difficult she will find it to understand. Big Wide Talk, an organization based in Cambridge which has engaged pre-school children and their parents in activities such as rock climbing, has discovered significant differences between even two- and three-year-olds in their ability to look ahead when weighing up risks. The older the children, the more they are able to understand the explanations of what might happen offered by those with expertise in the risks involved.

An alternative to well-informed guidance that allows children the degree of independence to which their skills are fitted is to teach them routines. Children too young to work out the possible consequences of an initial action by imagining the potential consequences are geared up to the adoption of routines. They lack the resistance to them that will come with growing self-confidence. Thus a routine like washing hands every time after using the toilet is one that is easily instilled and serves to protect the child before she is able (and needs) to understand the logic behind it.

Games

Imaginative play is a way of exploring the world. Rules may be laid down by adults, as in Paley's framework for such play in her kindergarten) or by the children themselves ('You be the baby and I'll be the mummy and you be sick and I have to give you medicine'). However, such rules must necessarily be limited in scope if exploration is to occur. Something different occurs when games with quite rigid and well-defined rules are introduced. A game such as musical chairs has an outcome that is unknown when the game starts and in one sense is very open. Nevertheless, the rules are rigid and may become more detailed if, for example, it has to be explained that pushing your friend off her chair is not allowed. All adult competitive sports have highly elaborated rules because the need to cover various contingencies has become clear in the course of their history. Games in which there is an element of overt competition and a set of rules to prevent this breaking down into less acceptable conflict are stories in the making, but the ways in which they can be developed are severely restricted. This stands in contrast to imaginative role play where Batman can confront witches, and police cars find their way to Sherwood Forest.

In the 1970s there was a strong reaction among playworkers against competitive games. While most such games operated on a team basis and had been justified on the grounds of the cooperation within teams that they encouraged, critical attention turned to the element of conflict between competing teams. There was a search for group games for children of primary school age that would encourage cooperation without introducing the element of contest with the outsider.

Games that were devised as part of this movement were successful in several respects. Where they often failed was in their lack of any clear climax. One of the things that makes competitive games attractive is that they give rise to well-structured narratives, but ones that cannot be described except in retrospect. Their ending is open at the start, but the ending is always clear. Even a draw is a clear result. There are also likely to be highs of excitement along the way, but all of these are linked to the end result.

In this respect the competitive game is a form of narrative that has a positive role in helping children to see sequences of events in narrative form. Like other narratives, they have clear openings and closures. They work most successfully when basic narrative competence has been achieved. Their place in work with children who have not got so far is more problematic in some respects, but it does exist. Any competitive game must be very simple if children under five are to understand it. There must be some attempt to distinguish between the rules of a game and routine, otherwise children may treat the game as an enjoyable but slightly puzzling ritual. Everyone knows the child who often asks to play hide and seek, but enjoys being found more than any other aspect of the game. In settings that have experimented with egg and spoon races using real eggs children have assumed that the purpose of the game is to be the first to drop your egg and see it make a satisfying splat on the ground. Initial misunderstanding of competition by many of the children has to be accepted, but, if there is some emphasis on the competitive element, children will begin to grasp the narrative that is being constructed. This, in turn, means that the limitations to the conflict have to be made clear.

Individual records

All settings keep records on children. The better the setting, the more effectively these will be shared with parents, so their basic format must be designed in ways that facilitate this. Relatively little use has been made so far of new technology in the form of websites and parent access to a setting's databases, although such moves have the potential to significantly enhance parental use of record systems. Effective sharing with parents means giving them opportunities to contribute to the record-keeping as well as to see the outcomes. The best settings have usually managed this. However, it is rare for children to be involved in the way their parents may be even in those settings that have taken cooperation with parents furthest. In addition to the fact that most children will only be at the beginning stages of literacy, the records will probably be maintained in ways that would be foreign to them even if they were literate.

Records do not need to be kept entirely in written form. Often those caring for children measure their height at regular intervals against the same surface, so that marks on that surface provide a visible and easily read record of the child's rate of physical growth, and the child's cooperation is required for this to happen. Such charts can be created and maintained within early years settings.

We need to consider ways in which this kind of idea can be extended. What kind of records can be developed to which children themselves can contribute? This is the sort of initiative that can be defended on the grounds of children's rights or the general democratic value of fostering participation by all those who form part of any social unit. There can be no quarrel with that, but the case put forward here is based on the child's need to situate herself ever more clearly in her own history. This is just as important as the use of mirrors to foster self-awareness in some of the settings in Reggio Emilia and elsewhere. Neither practice need exclude the other. The culture of which the setting forms part will tend to shape the form of self-awareness that is considered most valuable. Much of the child's understanding of her own history will come from discussion with those who are closest to her. It may also come at a later stage from fiction and from the kind of game many seven-year-olds play of pretending to be babies, something that is usually not a form of regression or even nostalgia, but a way of marking with pleasure the extent to which growth has taken place. The amusement such games bring comes from a sense of triumph. Adults do not want to grow older. Children do.

Formal records are a way of marking a child's progress and, therefore, a good setting will use some forms of recording that the children can understand and to which they can contribute, just as their parents may be able to use and contribute to other forms of recording. Among the elements of such recording can be

- visual representations of physical growth in terms of height, weight, etc.
- a timeline showing key events in which the child participated at the setting, these being selected by the children as well as staff or parents
- photographic records of personal participation in key events or of things the child has done
- things produced by the child kept with brief notes that might serve to trigger memory of their construction at later dates
- visual self-description and photographs of favourite things inside and outside the setting and of key people in the child's life with some format for designating those who may no longer be there, such as staff who have left
- sound or camcorder records of the child's perceptions at different times.

Some of these types of records could take up considerable space. ICT can provide a means of keeping them in ways that are easily accessible to the children as well as space saving. Visual and sound records are likely to seem especially important with children who are not yet literate, but it is possible to find equivalents for children who are visually or hearing impaired, such as measurement charts with markings that can be felt.

The setting's own stories

The setting itself will have its own stories and these provide a necessary counterpoint to the child's focus on herself, which has been the subject of most of this chapter.

Narrative self-description and understanding are rare for settings. They plan for the future. If they look back on their past it tends to be in terms of either celebration of particular events (including artificial ones such as the tenth anniversary of having started) or overall evaluation of what they have achieved in statistical or similar terms rather than in the construction of a narrative. If the staff themselves do not reflect on what has happened to their setting in narrative terms, they are unlikely to engage the children in such work.

There are four ways in which settings can begin to record their own stories with the children.

The first step is to make explicit the routine under which the setting operates. Routines facilitate organization, and their value in giving security and assurance to children is widely recognized. Nevertheless, not all settings are explicit about their routine with the children or, if they are, this arises casually as explanation of what is happening at a particular point of the day. This is in spite of the fact that the child's identification of routine is one of the necessary preliminaries to the development of narrative competence. With little or no prompting from the adults in her life, Emily in her bedtime monologues defined routines even for unusual events such as her visit to the airport (Nelson, 1989). In settings, and in particular in work with two- and three-year-olds, making routines explicit and asking the children to confirm their understanding of them could play an important part in laying the basis for narrative competence.

Special themes and projects provide an opportunity for the real development of a narrative understanding of what is happening. The use of a particular theme across the whole of a term or the celebration of a particular festival is something additional to the routine of activity, although perfectly compatible with it. Such activity has a clear beginning and end. A story can be made of it. The settings of Reggio Emilia have made this an essential part of their approach. What is important in what they have done is to engage children as well as staff fully in developing an understanding of the story of a particular project.

Projects can be seen as special entities around which stories can be built. They have a limited life span, which is fairly easy for children of three and upwards to comprehend. There may be more difficulty in helping the children to see themselves as part of an age cohort, to look at what has happened to their group from the time of entering the setting to the point at which they may leave it. Of course, this will be easier if there is a reasonable level of stability in the child group within a setting and if the great majority of children in any one cohort join at round about the same time. Even so, this is not a perspective that will occur to the children naturally. It could be addressed in circle time and other contexts. The need for children to understand their own history also suggests that more effort should be put into arranging contact between different age groups in settings. Fears that older children, with their greater abilities and sizes, will overwhelm the younger children, perhaps even bully them, have a basis in reality. Apart from this, the widespread practice of total separation of age groups in settings has its roots in the isolated individual model of child development and the assumption often made that the child must struggle to reach each cognitive stage on her own. This has been reinforced by occasionally excessive application of regulations about different space and staffing standards for different age groups. The basis for such standards is realistic, although they do not merit the almost iconic status they have acquired, which often impedes any sensible discussion of possible review. The fear of childcare inspectors that any relaxation on their part will encourage settings to mix age groups for reasons that are related purely to their own convenience and profits is also realistic. That said, it has become increasingly clear in recent years that older siblings and other children with whom they come into contact play key roles in the social and cognitive abilities of pre-school children. Planned contact between age groups is a relatively unexplored area in most British settings. More could be done. Such contact could help develop children's sense of their own age situation.

The idea that the setting itself has a story is one that will be most difficult for pre-school children to grasp. Their need for certainty and the small time scales on which they judge things inevitably mean that they will see their settings as being in some sense eternally given. However, occasionally key events will take place in the life of a setting – special anniversaries, change of lead manager, move to new premises or extension of the existing premises. Parents are usually involved in discussions about such events. It is less common for children to be fully involved. The greater their achieved level of narrative competence, the stronger the possibility of discussing with them the significance of such changes in the history of the setting. Any understanding of this they are able to achieve is a key step towards their being able to see themselves as living in a wider society with a historical dimension.

There are five things that must happen if work on helping children understand the story of what is happening to them at a setting is to go forward:

- The work must be based on a constantly revised understanding of the level of narrative competence achieved by each individual child. It is too easy to over- or underestimate the child's understanding in this respect.
- It must be based on explicit discussion with the children. It cannot be assumed that their understanding will develop naturally. Relevant statements made by children must be recorded and fed back to them at appropriate points. Discussion must not happen casually, but, like all narration, must be clearly marked in some way.
- The work of constructing narratives about the setting must happen as it proceeds. Maintenance of timelines or other devices has to be an integral part of the work.
- Once a project has finished or a significant stage in something has been reached, there is a need to speak about what has happened, to make a story of it, while inviting children to add to or modify that story in other ways so that its full significance can emerge.
- Documentation, including visual and sound records, must be maintained so that the story can be revised if necessary. If a particular festival is usually celebrated in a setting, then the planning for the next celebration can begin with a reflection by staff, parents and at least the older children on the previous year's experience.

Conclusion

The model that contrasts narrative and paradigmatic as ways of understanding the world tends to regard narrative in terms of fiction and imagination in the most romantic sense. If narrative competence is seen as a key element in cognitive development, then its importance has to be wider than this. Narrative also operates in the everyday world. We spend our lives swimming in a sea of stories of which fictional narrative is only one aspect. Attention to narrative in the early years curriculum should include all aspects of the children's care and education. It should not be pushed aside by focus on the paradigmatic or by the assumption that narrative is a matter of imaginative fiction alone.

Conclusion

The central thesis of this book is that narrative competence – the ability to understand and construct stories – is a more complex matter than it is often assumed to be and, therefore, that it deserves more attention in the planning of pre-school education.

To make this case I have called upon a number of academic disciplines to illustrate that complexity. Recent studies of memory in adults demonstrate that memories are frequently constructions rather than straightforward impressions left by experience. The ability to make such constructions is typical of the great majority of human children, but it is an achievement that develops over time, particularly in the period between the second and sixth birthdays. The construction of stories is not as straightforward a business as might be imagined. Since the mid-1960s narratologists have drawn attention to previously obscured issues. Anthropologists have demonstrated that conventions are important, especially when narration takes place in oral rather than written form. Conventions not only help to structure the narrative, but indicate that it is one, that it is a construction. The role of such conventions indicates that narrative competence has a cultural dimension. It cannot be seen in terms of a supposedly universal model of individual development.

Children's stories are now something separate from other fiction, but understanding of them is still overshadowed by judgement of them from a literary, therefore adult, point of view. This is particularly problematic in the case of stories composed for very young children. Finally, it has been argued that narrative cannot be seen in terms of fiction alone. This becomes clearer when the narrative dimension not just of history, but also of the natural sciences, is considered. The cognitive dimension of narrative competence is crucial.

The material that has been drawn from several fields enables us to sketch a picture of narrative competence and the process of its development in the young child. This book does not go much further than that. It offers neither a fully elaborated theoretical model nor a piece of original research of my own. On the other hand, it does offer reasons for believing in the central thesis outlined at the beginning of this concluding chapter.

The three chapters on daily practice in settings draw on the material outlined in the earlier part of the book. It is true that many of the ideas will be familiar to practitioners. There is much to be learned from careful observation of children and the application of experience. It might be argued, therefore, that the earlier chapters were unnecessary. I would counter that, apart from the intrinsic interest of the topics discussed, there is a need for greater familiarity with that body of theory. Without such knowledge it is easy to forget the lessons of experience and overlook the place that stories have in the cognitive development of the young child.

It is the cognitive aspect of narrative competence that has been the subject in hand. The term is employed here in a wider sense than it is by Fox (1993), from whom it is borrowed, since her focus was on children's response to literary form. The way in which it is used in this book also contrasts with the tendency to speak about stories for children as a means of escape from the realm of thought into the imagination, as a kind of holiday of the mind before returning to the daily grind. One of the objectives of the book has been to see narrative and the paradigmatic as both being methods of reaching beyond the dominant present in order to construct models that will help explain the universe in which we live, as being similar to each other as well as different, as both entailing a separation of their procedures from lived experience.

Emphasis on the cognitive aspect of narrative has inevitably meant downplaying the aspects of creativity, leisure and affect. This has been in a quest to restore the balance. Too often in the literature of child development attention to the cognitive aspect of something appears to require a deadly seriousness. In the 1970s when early years practitioners began to speak of the play of the young child as her form of work, three-quarters of a century after Groos (1901) proclaimed that insight, you could almost hear the sighs of relief. If it was work, then it was OK after all; they were not just mucking about. The kind of dismal puritanism that is not content with distinguishing between reason and emotion, work and play, but sets up conflict between them, is the last thing this book should be seen to endorse. Those whose work is most effective enjoy it as play. Any attempt to make a rigid separation between our ability to see abiding patterns, construct stories or use imagination always leads to disaster.

This is something the most creative minds, including scientists, have always known. Asked once by the mother of a young child what she should give her son to read to enhance the chances of his becoming an able scientist, Albert Einstein replied, 'Fairy stories.' Asked what he should read once he had got beyond that phase of childhood, the great man replied after a long pause for thought, 'More fairy stories.'

Bibliography

Andrade, J. (ed.) (2001) *Working Memory in Perspective*, London: Psychology Press.

Applebee, A. (1978) *The Child's Concept of Story: Ages Two to Seventeen*, Chicago: University of Chicago Press.

Arzipe, E. and Styles, M. (2003) *Children Reading Pictures: Interpreting Visual Texts*, London: RoutledgeFalmer.

Augustine (1955) 'On the Trinity', in J. Burnaby (trans. and ed.) *Augustine: Later Works*, Volume VIII of *The Library of Church Classics*, London: SCM Press.

Augustine (1960) *The Confessions*, trans. E.B. Pusey, New York: Washington Square Press.

Augustine (1972) *Concerning the City of God against the Pagans*, trans. H. Betterson, London: Penguin Books.

Baddley, A. (1986) *Working Memory*, Oxford: Clarendon Press.

Baker, A. and Greene, E. (1987) *Storytelling: Art and Technique*, 2nd edition, London: R.R. Bowker.

Barbour, J. (2000) *The End of Time: the Next Revolution in Our Understanding of the Universe*, London: Phoenix.

Barthes, R. (1973) *Le plaisir du texte*, Paris: Seuil.

Barthes, R. (1996) 'Introduction to the Structural Analysis of Narratives', trans. S. Heath, in S. Oriega and J.A. García Landa (eds) *Narratology: an Introduction*, London: Longman, 46–60.

Barthes, R. (1999) 'The Death of the Author', in D. Lodge (ed.) *Modern Criticism and Theory*, 2nd edition, London: Longman, 146–51.

Bartlett, F.C. (1950) *Remembering: a Study in Experimental and Social Psychology*, 2nd edition, Cambridge: Cambridge University Press.

Bauer, P.J. (1997) 'Development of Memory in Early Childhood', in N. Cowan (ed.) *The Development of Memory in Childhood*, Hove: Psychology Press, 83–111.

Beer, G. (1983) *Darwin's Plots: Evolutionary Narrative in Darwin, George Eliot and Nineteenth-Century Fiction*, London: Routledge and Kegan Paul.

Bettelheim, B. (1976) *The Uses of Enchantment: the Meaning and Importance of Fairy Tales*, London: Thames and Hudson.

Bornstein, M.H., Cote, L.R., Mastal, S., Painter, K., Park, S.-Y., Pasual, L., Pêcheux, M.-G., Ruel, J., Venuti, P. and Vyt, A. (2004) 'Cross-Linguistic Analyses of Vocabulary in Young Children: Spanish, Dutch, French, Hebrew, Italian, Korean and American English', *Child Development* 75 (4): 1115–39.

Boucher, J. (2001) '"Lost in a Sea of Time": Time-Parsing and Autism', in C. Hoerl and T. McCormack (eds) *Time and Memory: Issues in Philosophy and Psychology*, Oxford: Clarendon Press, 111–35.

Bowman, I. (1972) *Lewis Carroll as I Knew Him*, New York: Dover Publications.

Bremond, C. (1996) 'The Logic of Narrative Possibilities', in S. Oriega and J.A. García Landa (eds) *Narratology: an Introduction*, London: Longman, 62–75.

Broadbent, D.E. (1958) *Perception and Communication*, London: Pergamon Press.

Brock, A. (1999) *Into the Enchanted Forest: Language, Drama and Science in Primary Schools*, Stoke-on-Trent: Trentham Books.

Brooks, P. (1984) *Reading for the Plot*, Oxford: Clarendon Press.

Browne, N. (1999) *Young Children's Literacy Development and the Role of Television Texts*, London: Falmer Press.

Bruner, J. (1986) *Actual Minds, Possible Worlds*, Cambridge, Mass.: Harvard University Press.

Bruner, J. (1990) *Acts of Meaning*, Cambridge, Mass.: Harvard University Press.

Carey, P. (2000) *Augustine's Invention of the Inner Self: the Legacy of a Christian Platonist*, Oxford: Oxford University Press.

Carr, E.H. (1962) *What is History?*, London: Macmillan.

Carter, R. (2000) *Mapping the Mind*, London: Phoenix Paperbacks.

Cassidy, K.W., Fineberg, D.S., Brown, K. and Perkins, A. (2005) 'Theory of Mind May Be Contagious, But You Don't Catch It from Your Twin', *Child Development* 76 (1): 97–106.

Chomsky, N. (1968) *Language and Mind*, New York: Harcourt Brace Jovanovich.

Cleevemans, A. (1997) 'Principles for Implicit Learning', in D.C. Berry (ed.) *How Implicit Is Implicit Learning?*, Oxford: Oxford University Press, 195–234.

Colwell, E. (1980) *Storytelling*, London: Bodley Head.

Conway, M. (1995) *Flashbulb Memories*, Hove: Lawrence Erlbaum Associates.

Cooper, H. (1995) *History in the Early Years*, London: Routledge.

Cooper, P. (1993) *When Stories Come to School: Telling, Writing and Performing Stories in the Early Childhood Classroom*, New York: Teachers and Writers Collaborative.

Cott, J. (1984) *Pipers at the Gates of Dawn: the Wisdom of Children's Literature*, Harmondsworth: Viking Books.

Cotton, P. (2000) *Picture Books sans Frontières*, Stoke-on-Trent: Trentham Books.

Cox, M. (1992) *Children's Drawings*, London: Penguin Books.

Culler, J. (1975) 'Defining Narrative Units', in R. Fowler (ed.) *Style and Structure in Literature: Essays in the New Stylistics*, Oxford: Basil Blackwell, 123–42.

Darton, F.J.H. (1982) *Children's Books in England: Five Centuries of Social Life*, 3rd (revised) edition, Cambridge: Cambridge University Press.

Davies, B. (1989) *Frogs and Snails and Feminist Tales: Pre-school Children and Gender*, Sydney: Allen and Unwin.

Davies, P. (1995) *About Time: Einstein's Unfinished Revolution*, London: Penguin Books.

Dockrell, J., Stuart, M. and King, D. (2004) *'Talking Time': Supporting Effective Practice in Pre-school Provision*, London: Institute of Education.

Dokic, J., (2001) 'Is Memory Purely Preservative?', in C. Hoerl and T. McCormack (eds) *Time and Memory: Issues in Philosophy and Psychology*, Oxford: Clarendon Press, 213–32.

Dundas, A. (1965) 'On Computers and Folklore', *Western Folklore* 29: 185–9.

Dunn, J. (1988) *The Beginnings of Social Understanding*, Cambridge, Mass.: Harvard University Press.

Edelman, G.M. (1989) *The Remembered Present: a Biological Theory of Consciousness*, New York: Basic Books.

Edelman, G.M. (2004) *Wider than the Sky: the Phenomenal Gift of Consciousness*, London: Allen Lane.

Engel, L. (2002) 'Paws for Thought', *Nursery World* 3812: 22–3.

Engel, L. (2003a) 'All at Sea', *Nursery World* 3847: 16–17.

Engel, L. (2003b) 'It's a Gift', *Nursery World* 3878: 24–5.

Engel, S. (1995a) *Context Is Everything: the Nature of Memory*, New York: W.F. Freeman.

Engel, S. (1995b) *The Stories Children Tell: Making Sense of the Narratives of Childhood*, New York: W.H. Freeman.

Evans, J. (ed.) (1998) *What's in the Picture? Responding to Illustrations in Picture Books*, London: Paul Chapman.

Fivush, R. (ed.) (1994) *Long-term Retention of Infant Memories*, special edition of the journal *Memory* 2 (4).

Fivush, R. and Hudson, J.A. (eds) (1990) *Knowing and Remembering in Young Children*, Cambridge: Cambridge University Press.

Fivush, R., Pipe, M.-E., Murachver, T. and Reese, E. (1997) 'Events Spoken and Unspoken: Implications of Language and Memory Development for the Recovered Memory Debate', in M.A. Conway (ed.) *Recovered Memories and False Memories*, Oxford: Oxford University Press, 34–62.

Fludernik, M. (1996) *Towards a 'Natural' Narratology*, London: Routledge.

Fodor, J.A. (1993) *The Modularity of Mind: an Essay on Faculty Psychology*, Cambridge, Mass.: Bradford Books/MIT Press.

Forster, E.M. (1993) *Aspects of the Novel*, London: Hodder and Stoughton.

Fowler, R. (1977) *Linguistics and the Novel*, London: Methuen.

Fox, C. (1993) *At the Very Edge of the Forest: the Influence of Literature on Storytelling by Children*, London: Cassell.

Freud, S. (1953) *Three Essays on the Theory of Sexuality*, the Standard Edition of the Complete Psychological Works of Sigmund Freud, Volume VII, London: Hogarth Press, 135–243.

Freud, S. (1955) *Beyond the Pleasure Principle*, the Standard Edition of the Complete Psychological Works of Sigmund Freud, Volume XVIII, London: Hogarth Press, 7–64.

Gaunt, C. (2003) 'Toy Story', *Nursery World* 3872: 24.

Gibbon, E. (1914) *The Decline and Fall of the Roman Empire*, ed. J.B. Bury, London: Methuen.

Glen, C.G. (1978) 'The Role of Episodic Structure and of Story Length in Children's Recall of Simple Stories', *Journal of Verbal Learning and Verbal Behavior* 17: 229–47.

Goldthwaite, J. (1980) 'Notes on the Children's Book Trade: All Is Not Well in Tinsel Town', in S. Eggott, G.T. Stubbs and L.F. Ashley (eds) *Only Connect: Readings in Children's Literature*, Oxford: Oxford University Press, 389–404.

Gopnik, A. (1984) 'The Acquisition of "Gone" and the Development of the Object Concept', *Journal of Child Language* 9: 303–18.

Gopnik, A., Meltzoff, A. and Kuhl, P. (1999) *How Babies Think*, London: Orion Books.

Graham, J. (1998) 'Turning the Visual into the Verbal: Children Reading Wordless Books', in J. Evans (ed.) *What's in the Picture?*, London: Paul Chapman, 25–43.

Groos, K. (1901) *The Play of Man*, London: Heinemann.

Grugeon, E. and Gardner, P. (2000) *The Art of Storytelling for Teachers and Pupils: Using Stories to Develop Literacy in Primary Classrooms*, London: David Fulton.

Gurney, K. (1997) *An Introduction to Neural Networks*, London: VCL Press.

Hawking, S. (1995) *A Brief History of Time: From the Big Bang to Black Holes*, New York: Bantam Press.

Hilton, M., Styles, M. and Watson, V. (eds) (1997) *Opening the Nursery Door: Reading, Writing and Childhood 1600–1900*, London: Routledge.

Howe, M.L., Cichetti, D., Toth, S.L. and Cerrito, B.M. (2004) 'True and False Memories in Maltreated Children', *Child Development* 75 (5): 1407–17.

Hymes, D. (1996) *Ethnography, Linguistics, Narrative Inequality: Towards an Understanding of Voice*, London: Taylor and Francis.

James, W. (1890) *Principles of Psychology*, New York: Henry Holt.

Jean, G. (1979) *Les voies de l'imaginaire enfantin: les contes, les poèmes, le réel*, Paris: Éditions du Scarabée.

Jean, G. (1981) *Le pouvoir des contes*, Paris: Casterman.

John, T. (1989) 'Children's Historical Fiction and a Sense of the Past', in D. Atkinson (ed.) *The Children's Bookroom: Reading and the Use of Books*, Stoke-on-Trent: Trentham Books, 101–6.

Johnson, G. (1992) *In the Palaces of Memory: How We Build the Worlds Inside Our Heads*, London: Grafton (HarperCollins).

Kanner, L. (1943) 'Autistic Disturbances of Affective Contact', *Nervous Child* 2: 217–50.

Karmiloff-Smith, A. (1992) *Beyond Modularity: a Developmental Perspective on Cognitive Science*, Cambridge, Mass.: MIT Press.

Kerby, A.P. (1991) *Narrative and the Self*, Bloomington: Indiana University Press.

Kesner, R.P. (1998) 'Neurobiological Views of Memory', in J.L. Martinez and R.P. Kesner (eds) *Neurobiology of Learning and Memory*, London: Academic Press.

Kitson, N. (1994) '"Please Miss Alexander: Will You Be the Robber?" Fantasy Play: a Case for Adult Intervention', in J.R. Moyles (ed.) *The Excellence of Play*, Buckingham: Open University Press, 88–98.

Kleinknecht, E. and Beike, D.R. (2004) 'How Knowing and Doing Inform an Autobiography: Theory of Mind, Narrative and Event Memory Skills', *Applied Cognitive Psychology* 18: 745–64.

Kozulin, A. (1990) *Vygotsky's Psychology: A Biography of Ideas*, London: Harvester Wheatsheaf.

Labov, W. (1972) *Language in the Inner City: Studies in the Black English Vernacular*, Oxford: Basil Blackwell.

Langair, M. (ed.) (1997) *The Large, the Small and the Human Mind*, Cambridge: Cambridge University Press.

Launer, J. (2002) *Narrative-based Primary Care: a Practical Guide*, Oxford: Radcliffe Medical Press.

Le Doux, J. (1996) *The Emotional Brain*, New York: Simon and Schuster.

Lévi-Strauss, C. (1964) *Mythologiques I: Le Cru et le cuit*, Paris: Plon.

Lévi-Strauss, C. (1966) *Mythologiques II: Du miel aux cendres*, Paris: Plon.

Lévi-Strauss, C. (1968) *Mythologiques III: L'Origine des manières de table*, Paris: Plon.

Lévi-Strauss, C. (1971) *Mythologiques IV: L'Homme nu*, Paris: Plon.

Lévi-Strauss, C. (1984) 'Structure and Form: Reflections on a Work by Vladimir Propp', trans. M. Layton, in V. Propp (ed.) *Theory and History of Folklore*, Minneapolis: University of Minnesota Press, 167–88.

Lewis, C.S. (1980) 'On Three Ways of Writing for Children', in S. Egott, G.T. Stubbs and L.F. Ashley (eds) *Only Connect: Readings on Children's Literature*, Oxford: Oxford University Press 207–20.

Lewis, D. (2001) *Reading Contemporary Picturebooks: Picturing Text*, London: RoutledgeFalmer.

Libet, B. (2004) *Mind Time: the Temporal Factor in Consciousness*, Cambridge, Mass.: Harvard University Press.

Lord, A.B. (1960) *The Singer of Tales*, Cambridge, Mass.: Harvard University Press.

Loveland, K. and Tunali, B. (1993) 'Narrative Language in Autism and the Theory of Mind Hypothesis: a Wider Perspective', in S. Baron-Cohen, H. Tager-Flusberg and D.J. Cohen (eds) *Understanding Other Minds: Perspectives from Autism*, Oxford: Oxford University Press.

Luria, A.R. (1969) *The Mind of a Mnemonist*, trans. L. Soloratoff, London: Jonathan Cape.

Medlicott, M. (2001) 'All about Storytelling', *Nursery World* 101: 15–22.

Moffett, J. (1983) *Teaching the Universe of Discourse*, 2nd edition, Portsmouth, NH: Boynton/Cook Publishers.

Montessori, M. (1936) *The Secret of Childhood*, trans. B.B. Carter, Banbury: Orient Longman.

Mortimer, P. (1980) 'Thoughts Concerning Children's Books', in S. Eggott, G.T. Stubbs and L.F. Ashley (eds) *Only Connect: Readings in Children's Literature*, Oxford: Oxford University Press, 101–10.

Moscovitch, M. (ed.) (1984) *Infant Memory: Its Relation to Normal and Pathological Memory in Humans and Other Animals*, London: Plenum Press.

Moscovitch, M. (1985) 'Memory from Infancy to Old Age: Implications for Theories of Normal and Pathological Memory', *Annals of the New York Academy of Sciences* 444: 78–96.

Murdoch, I. (1997) 'Against Dryness', in P. Conradi (ed.) *Existentialists and Mystics: Writings on Philosophy and Literature by Iris Murdoch*, London: Chatto and Windus, 287–95.

Nadel, L. and Zola-Morgan, S. (1984) 'Infantile Amnesia: a Neurobiological Perspective', in M. Moscovitch (ed.) *Infant Memory: Its Relation to Normal and Pathological Memory in Humans and Other Animals*, London: Plenum Press, 145–72.

Nelson, K. (ed.) (1989) *Narratives from the Crib*, Cambridge, Mass.: Harvard University Press.

Nicholson, H.N. (1996) *Place in Story Time: Geography through Stories at Key Stages 1 and 2*, 2nd edition, London: The Geographical Association.

Oakhill, J. (1995) 'Development in Reading', in V. Lee and P.D. Gupta (eds) *Children's Cognitive and Language Development*, Oxford: Blackwell in association with the Open University, 269–99.

Olrik, A. (1992) 'The Structure of Narrative: The Epic Laws', in A. Olrik, *Principles for Oral Narrative Research*, trans. K. Wolf and J. Jensen, Bloomington: Indiana University Press, 41–61.

Oriega, S. and García Landa, J.A. (eds) (1996) *Narratology: an Introduction*, London: Longman.

Pace, D. (1982) 'Beyond Morphology: Lévi-Strauss and the Analysis of Folklore', in A. Dundas (ed.) *Cinderella: a Casebook*, London: University of Wisconsin Press.

Page, M. (2000) 'Connectionist Modelling in Psychology: a Localist Manifesto', *Behavioral and Brain Sciences* 23 (4): 443–512.

Paley, V.G. (1981) *Wally's Stories: Conversations in the Kindergarten*, Cambridge, Mass.: Harvard University Press.

Paley, V.G. (1990) *The Boy Who Would Be a Helicopter: the Uses of Storytelling in the Classroom*, Cambridge, Mass.: Harvard University Press.

Penrose, R. (1990) *The Emperor's New Mind: Concerning Computers, Minds and the Laws of Physics*, Oxford: Vintage Books/Oxford University Press.

Penrose, R. (1995) *Shadows of the Mind: a Search for the Missing Science of Consciousness*, Oxford: Vintage Books/Oxford University Press.

Perner, J. (1991) *Understanding the Representational Mind*, Cambridge, Mass: MIT Press.

Perris, E., Myers, N. and Clifton, R. (1990) 'Long Term Memory for a Single Infancy Experience', *Child Development* 61: 1796–807.

Piaget, J. (1960) *The Child's Conception of the World*, trans. J. and A. Adams, Paterson, NJ: Littlefield, Adams and Co.

Piaget, J. (2002) *The Language and Thought of the Child*, trans. M. and R. Gabain, London: Routledge.

Pičević, E. (1990) *Change and Selves*, Oxford: Clarendon Press.

Pillemer, D.B. and White, S.H. (1989) 'Childhood Events Recalled by Children and Adults', in H.W. Reese (ed.) *Advances in Child Development and Behavior*, Volume 21, London: Academic Press, 297–340.

Pitcher, E.G. and Prelinger, E. (1963) *Children Tell Stories: an Analysis of Fantasy*, New York: International Universities Press.

Prigogine, I. (1980) *From Being to Becoming*, San Francisco: W.H. Freeman.

Prigogine, I. (1996) *The End of Certainty: Time, Chaos and the New Laws of Nature*, New York: The Free Press.

Prince, G. (1973) *A Grammar of Stories*, The Hague: Mouton.

Prince, G. (1982) *Narratology*, The Hague: Mouton.

Propp, V. (1968) *Morphology of the Folktale*, trans. L. Scott, Austin: University of Texas Press.

Propp, V. (1984) 'The Structural and Historical Study of the Wondertale', trans. S. Shishkoff, in V. Propp (ed.) *Theory and History of Folklore*, Minneapolis: University of Minnesota Press, 67–81.

Protheroe, P. (1992) *Vexed Texts: How Children's Picture Books Promote Illiteracy*, Lewes, Sussex: The Book Guild.

Qin, J., Quas, J.A., Redlich, A.D. and Goodman, G.S. (1997) 'Children's Eyewitness Testimony: Memory Development in the Legal Context', in N. Cowan (ed.) *The Development of Memory in Childhood*, Hove: Psychology Press, 301–41.

Qualifications and Curriculum Authority (QCA) (2000) *Curriculum Guidance for the Foundation Stage*, London: Department for Education and Employment (DfEE).

Ray, W. (1990) *Story and History: Narrative Authority and Social Identity in the Eighteenth-century French and English Novel*, Oxford: Basil Blackwell.

Reber, A.S. (1993) *Implicit Learning and Tacit Knowledge: an Essay on Cognitive Unconsciousness*, Oxford: Oxford University Press.

Ricoeur, P. (1985) *Time and Narrative*, Vol. 2, trans. K. McLaughlin and D. Pellauer, Chicago: University of Chicago Press.

Robinson, M. (1997) *Children Reading Print and Television*, London: Falmer Press.

Rodari, G. (1973) *Grammatica della fantasia*, Turin: Einaudi.

Rose, R. and Philpot, T. (2004) *The Child's Own Story: Life Story Work with Traumatised Children*, London: Jessica Kingsley Publishers.

Rose, S. (1992) *The Making of Memory: from Molecules to Mind*, London: Bantam Press.

Rubin, D.C. (1995) *Memory in Oral Traditions: the Cognitive Psychology of Epic Ballads and Counting-Out Rhymes*, Oxford: Oxford University Press.

Schachter, D.L. and Moscovitch, M. (1984) 'Infants, Amnesics and Dissociable Memory Systems', in M. Moscovitch (ed.) *Infant Memory: Its Relation to Normal and Pathological Memory in Humans and Other Animals*, London: Plenum Press, 173–216.

Schillebeeckx, E. (1983) *Jesus: an Experiment in Christology*, trans. H. Hoskins, London: Collins/Fount Paperbacks.

Schiro, M.S. (2004) *Oral Storytelling and Teaching Mathematics: Pedagogical and Multicultural Perspectives*, London: Paul Chapman.

Seifert, W. (ed.) (1983) *Neurobiology of the Hippocampus*, London: Academic Press.

Sharit, Z. (1989) 'The Double Attribution of Texts for Children and How It Affects Writing for Children', in C.F. Otten and G.D. Schmidt (eds) *The Voice of the Narrator in Children's Literature: Insights from Writers and Critics*, New York: Greenwood Press, 85–97.

Sims, K. (1999) 'How Reliable Are Child Eyewitnesses?', *The Psychologist* 12 (4): 191.

Smith, P.K. (1984) 'The Relevance of Fantasy Play for Development in Young Children', in H. Cowie (ed.) *The Development of Children's Imaginative Writing*, London: Croom Helm, 12–31.

Spufford, F. (2002) *The Child That Books Built: a Memoir of Childhood and Reading*, London: Faber and Faber.

Steele, I. (1976) *Developments in History Teaching*, Shepton Mallet: Open Books.

Tannen, D. (1980) 'A Comparative Analysis of Oral Narrative Structures: Athenian Greek and American English', in W. Chafe (ed.) *The Pear Stories: Cognitive,*

Cultural and Linguistic Aspects of Narrative Production, Norwood, NJ: Norwood, 51–87.

Teachers in Development Education (2002) *Start with a Story: Supporting Young Children's Exploration of Issues*, 2nd edition, Birmingham: Birmingham Development Education Centre.

Thompson, C.P., Skowronski, J.J., Larsen, S.F. and Betz, A.L. (1996) *Autobiographical Memory: Remembering What and Remembering When*, Mahwah, NJ: Lawrence Erlbaum Associates.

Todorov, T. (ed.) (1965) *Théorie de la littérature: Textes des formalistes russes*, Paris: Éditions du Seuil.

Todorov, T. (1969) *Grammaire du Décaméron*, The Hague: Mouton.

Traça, M.E. (1992) *O fio da mémoria: do conto popular ao conto para crianças*, Oporto: Porto Editora.

Trigo Cutiño, J.M., Aller García, C., Garrote García, M. and Márquez Serrano, M. (1997) *El niño de hoy ante el cuento: investigación y aplicaciones didácticas*, Seville: Editorial Guadalmena.

Tsuda, I. (2001) 'Towards an Interpretation of Dynamic Neural Activity in Terms of Chaotic Dynamical Systems', *Behavioral and Brain Sciences* 27 (4): 491–541.

Tucker, N. (1981) *The Child and the Book: a Psychological and Literary Exploration*, Cambridge: Cambridge University Press.

Waldvogel, S. (1982) 'Childhood Memories', in U. Neisser (ed.) *Memory Observed: Remembering in Natural Contexts*, San Francisco: W.H. Freeman, 73–6.

Wall, B. (1991) *The Narrator's Voice: the Dilemma of Children's Fiction*, London: Macmillan Academic.

Wallschlager, J. (2000) *Hans Christian Andersen: the Life of a Storyteller*, London: Allen Lane/The Penguin Press.

Ward, L.O. (1976) 'History in the Middle Years', *Teaching History* IV (6): 359–62.

Watson, V. and Styles, M. (eds) (1996) *Talking Pictures: Pictorial Texts and Young Readers*, London: Hodder and Stoughton.

Wellman, H.M. (1990) *The Child's Theory of Mind*, Cambridge, Mass.: MIT Press.

Wetzler, S.E. and Sweeney, J.A. (1986) 'Childhood Amnesia: an Empirical Demonstration', in D.A. Rubin (ed.) *Autobiographical Memory*, Cambridge: Cambridge University Press, 191–201.

White, D. (1954) *Books Before Five*, Oxford: Oxford University Press.

White, M. and Epston, D. (1990) *Narrative Means to Therapeutic Ends*, New York: W.W. Norton.

Wood, D. (1998) *How Children Think and Learn: The Social Context of Cognitive Development*, 2nd edition, Oxford: Blackwell Publishing.

Children's stories referred to in the text

I have not included here either the traditional stories that have been re-edited for young children or classic children's books of the late nineteenth and early twentieth centuries by authors to whom I have made reference such as Lewis Carroll or A.A. Milne. These are nearly all widely available in a variety of editions. This list includes books intended for younger children published since 1960 to which reference is made in the text. In all cases the place of publication is London.

Raymond Briggs (1978) *The Snowman*, Hamish Hamilton.

Eileen Browne (2000) *Handa's Surprise*, Walker Books.

Eric Carle (1969) *The Very Hungry Caterpillar*, Hamish Hamilton.

Pat Hutchins (1970) *Rosie's Walk*, Bodley Head.

Judith Kerr (1968) *The Tiger Who Came to Tea*, HarperCollins.

Satoshi Kitamura (1987) *Lily Takes a Walk*, Blackie.

David Mills and Derek Brazell (1999) *Lima's Red Hot Chilli*, Mantra.

Jan Ormerod (1988) *The Story of Chicken Licken*, Walker Books.

Michael Rosen and Helen Oxenbury (1989) *We're Going on a Bear Hunt*, Walker Books.

John Scieska and Lane Smith (1972) *The True Story of the Three Little Pigs*, Viking.

Maurice Sendak (1967) *Where the Wild Things Are*, Bodley Head.

Jill Tomlinson (1968) *The Owl Who Was Afraid of the Dark*, Methuen.

Eugene Trivizas and Helen Oxenbury (1993) *The Three Little Wolves and the Big Bad Pig*, Heinemann.

Index